BATTLES OF THE
PROPHET

First published in the UK by Beacon Books and Media Ltd
Earl Business Centre, Dowry Street, Oldham, OL8 2PF, UK.

First edition published in 2023

www.beaconbooks.net

ISBN 978-1-915025-58-6 Paperback
ISBN 978-1-915025-59-3 Hardback
ISBN 978-1-915025-60-9 Ebook

Cataloging-in-Publication record for this book is available from the British Library

Cover design by Raees Mahmood Khan

BATTLES OF THE PROPHET

A Brief Guide to the Ghazawaat of the Prophet Muhammad

HALIMA BINT MUHAMMAD ABDUL HANNAN

BEACON BOOKS

SYRIA

Dawmat ul-Jandal

Tabuk

Khaybar

MADINAH

ARABIA

NUBIA

Red Sea

MAKKAH
Ta'if

ABYSSINIA
(Ethiopia)

YEMEN

MESOPOTAMIA
(Iraq)

PERSIA
(Iran)

Persian Gulf

Gulf of Oman

OMAN

CONTENTS

Arabian Sea

Dedicated to my mother

بِسْمِ ٱللّٰهِ ٱلرَّحْمٰنِ ٱلرَّحِيمِ

"Fight in the path of Allah, and fight those who fight against you.
But remember, not to go beyond the boundaries.
Allah dislikes those who cross the boundaries."
(Surah Baqarah: 190)

PREFACE

All praise be to Allah, who said, 'Muhammad is not the father of any of your men, but (he is) the Messenger of Allah, and the Seal of the Prophets: and Allah has full knowledge of all things.'[1] Peace and blessings be upon His Messenger Muhammad ﷺ who said, 'I am Muhammad, I am Ahmad. I am the remover and disbelief shall be erased through me; I am the assembler. People shall be assembled on the Day of Judgement after my time. I am the last in the matter and no Prophet shall succeed me.'[2] May the blessings of Allah be upon his companions, who followed in his footsteps and instilled the Qur'an and Sunnah in their lives. Everything comes from Allah and to Him we shall return. For Allah says, 'O you who believe! Obey Allah, and obey the Messenger.'[3] I witness that there is no god but Allah. I also witness that Muhammad ﷺ is His servant and His Messenger, who was sent as a mercy for all, a bearer of good news to the believers, and a warning for the deviators. Be obedient to Allah and His Messenger ﷺ. Remember Allah, and He will remember you.

The work before you is a concise book on the ghazawaat (battles) of Prophet Muhammad ﷺ and the historical context in which they took place. My primary focus is the events that

1 Surah Ahzab: 40.
2 *Muwatta Malik* 61/1861.
3 Surah Nisa: 59.

ix

occurred before and after each battle. It is unanimously agreed that the number of battles is 27, and this work seeks to discuss each battle in some detail.

My motivation to compile this book was my love for research and Islamic history. I wanted to make the ghazawaat accessible and easily comprehensible to English speakers. Although there is a large body of work in Arabic and Urdu in this area, there is a minimal amount in English. Thus, during my fourth year in the Alimiyyah studies, I embarked on this journey to collate details of the battles in one handbook. I have chosen a selection of Arabic commentaries as my main references throughout this process, in particular: *Sīrah ibn Hisham* and its commentary *Al-Rawd al-Unuf* alongside *Al-Rahīq ul-Makhtūm* and the commentary of Zarqāni. I have also consulted my teachers for further insight and guidance. By the grace of Allah and His mercy, after six years of going back and forth, I have completed the project. I am aware of my limitations and shortcomings in the field of Hadith literature, so whatever errors this book contains, I alone take responsibility for them. I hope and pray that Allah ﷻ blesses this humble effort and that it inspires others to delve deeper into the life of Prophet Muhammad ﷺ.

Halima Bint Muhammad Abdul Hannan
Student of Knowledge
1st Rabiʿ ath-Thani 1443AH

INTRODUCTION

Was Islam spread by the sword or *akhlāq* (character)? This question has intrigued and been debated by historians for centuries. Orientalist and non-orientalist historians have approached this question in different ways and different conclusions have been reached.

My hypothesis is that in determining whether Islam was spread by the sword, first, the following questions need to be answered: were the ghazawaat considered to be defensive or offensive? Was jihad a means to force people to convert to Islam? Was the sword used as a first or last resort when converting people to Islam? The term jihad is derived from the root word *juhud* which means to 'strive, endeavor, to burn out, to put out pains.' Jihad is the application of strength and striving to elevate the word of Allah; the highest form of jihad is battle and exertion of the soul. In battle, one exhausts themselves for the cause of Allah to show obedience to Him and to promote the religion without any worldly benefit. Jihad is mistakenly perceived as violence directed towards disbelievers; however, in reality, it is the struggle against all types of evil faced by an individual. It is important to note that if one wants to promote Allah's words then they should remain within the boundaries set by Allah and His Messenger ﷺ and live and act accordingly.

The concept of jihad and its sanctioning can be understood from the following verse from the Qur'an: 'Fight in the path of Allah, and fight those who fight against you. But remember, not to go beyond the boundaries. Allah dislikes those who cross the boundaries' (Qur'an, 2:190). The conditions of jihad and its restrictions can be derived from the aforementioned verse. Firstly, we are informed that jihad is only to be waged for the cause of Allah, not for materialistic or personal matters. Secondly, jihad is only to be only waged as an act of defence, against those who attack. Lastly, Allah reinforces the importance of not 'exceeding boundaries' within warfare.

This concept can be further understood from the hadith of Prophet Muhammad ﷺ when he says: 'Proceed in Allah's name, with Allah, and upon the religion of Allah's Prophet. Do not kill a feeble old man, a child, an infant or a woman. Do not be dishonest about the booty, collect your booty [share], do good and act correctly. For Allah loves those who act correctly.'[4]

All of the battles of Prophet Muhammad ﷺ could be considered defensive as they were in reaction to an instigation or aggression from the opposition. Prophet Muhammad ﷺ fought all battles against his kinsfolk and very few were fought against other communities and non-Arabs. The first call to battle was granted by Allah when He said: 'Permission to fight back has been granted to those being fought against, because they have been wronged' (Qur'an 22:39). However, after the Treaty of Hudaybiyah, the Muslims entered a new phase of warfare. Prophet Muhammad ﷺ declared after the battle of Qurayzah, 'From now on, we shall be the one to make war on them, not them on us' (Sahih Bukhari 3099). This was still a defensive war on the grounds that a battle can be considered so when it is fought to defend against the initiators of war. However, offensive battles were fought due to the aggression carried out by the initiators, the disbelievers. In response to this, an attack was launched to protect the Muslim population. In his book *Fiqh us-Sunnah*, Sheikh Muhammad Saeed al-Buti highlights the defensive wars as Badr, Qaynuqa,

4 *Sahih Muslim* 1731.

Uhud, Bi'r Maunah, Banu Nadir, Dhatur Riqa', Banu Mustaliq, Banu Qurayzah, and Khandaq. On the other hand, battles fought initially, like Abwa, Buwat, and Ushayrah, are classified as offensive battles.

An alternative view is that Islam was spread by the *akhlāq* (character) of Prophet Muhammad ﷺ, not the sword. If one looks carefully at the life of Prophet Muhammad ﷺ and the stories of many companions converting to Islam, one realizes that they accepted Islam of their own accord and out of amazement of the religion, such as Umar ؓ, Hamza ؓ, Mus'ab bin Umayr ؓ, Khalid bin Walīd ؓ and many more. Furthermore, one can also understand this from the etiquettes of war. Islam was never enforced upon an individual; rather, they were invited to the religion as mentioned in the Qur'an: 'There is no compulsion in religion. The right path is distinguishable from the wrong. Hence, he who rejects *taghut* (evil ones) and believes in Allah has indeed taken hold of the firm grasp. And Allah is All-Hearing and All-Knowing' (Qur'an 2:256). This point can be further proven from the numerous occasions that Prophet Muhammad ﷺ wrote letters to governors or kings inviting them to Islam, alongside suggesting a peace treaty.

However, if all conditions are disregarded and the opposition outwardly cause harm to the Muslims and the religion of Allah, then, and only then, is war waged against them. This procedure has also been mentioned in the Qur'an, 'Invite (people) to the Way of Allah with wisdom and kind advice and only debate with them in the best manner' (Qur'an 16:125). Furthermore, in Surah Anfāl, Allah educates the Muslims regarding the etiquettes of jihad: 'O you who believe, when you meet a group of enemies, be firm, and remember Allah a lot, so that you may be successful. Obey Allah and His Messenger. And do not dispute; you will lose courage and then your strength will depart. Be patient; indeed Allah is with the patient.'[5]

5 Surah Anfal: 45-46.

Here, Allah has highlighted five principles of warfare:

1. To be firm and steadfast when confronted with the enemy. This requires holding the ground both physically and mentally.

2. To have *tawakkul* (reliance) on Allah and to remember Him immensely at this time. The remembrance of Allah is the spiritual weapon for a believer as it allows them to hold their ground.

3. To conform to the commandments of Allah and His Messenger ﷺ. Negligence and disobedience in the commands of Allah are the causes of deprivation of His blessings and His displeasure.

4. To promote unity amongst each other as this will enhance dominance and strength. Avoid quarrels as they breed cowardice. Unity strengthens a group and each member is heightened by the positive force.

5. To be patient, as Allah loves the patient.

GHAZWAH ABWA

This was the first military campaign that Prophet Muhammad ﷺ took part in, the last being Tabuk. Prophet Muhammad ﷺ appointed Sa'd bin Ubadah as his vicegerent of Madinah. The flag of the battle was held by Hamza ﷺ.

Other names:	Waddan
Date:	Beginning of Safar 2AH
Opposition:	Quraysh and the Banu Damrah
No. of Muslims:	Sixty Muhajirun
Prominent figures:	Unknown
No. of Unbelievers:	Unknown
Prominent figures:	Unknown
Outcome:	No physical combat

Al-Abwa is a village thirteen miles from al-Juhfah, which is in the eastern direction of Madinah.[6] According to another opinion, it is twenty-three miles from al-Juhfah.[7] However, it is specifically mentioned that Abwa is a valley from the valleys of Hijaz, within which many wells exist. The area is known as Khuraybah[8] in the present day. The expedition of Abwa is also known as Waddan, possibly because these two areas are six miles apart.[9] According to

6 *Fathul-Bari, Kitaab-ul-Maghazi* 7/349.
7 Ibid.
8 *Al-Rawd al-Unuf*, 3/33-34.
9 *Fathul-Bari, Kitaab-ul-Maghazi* 7/349.

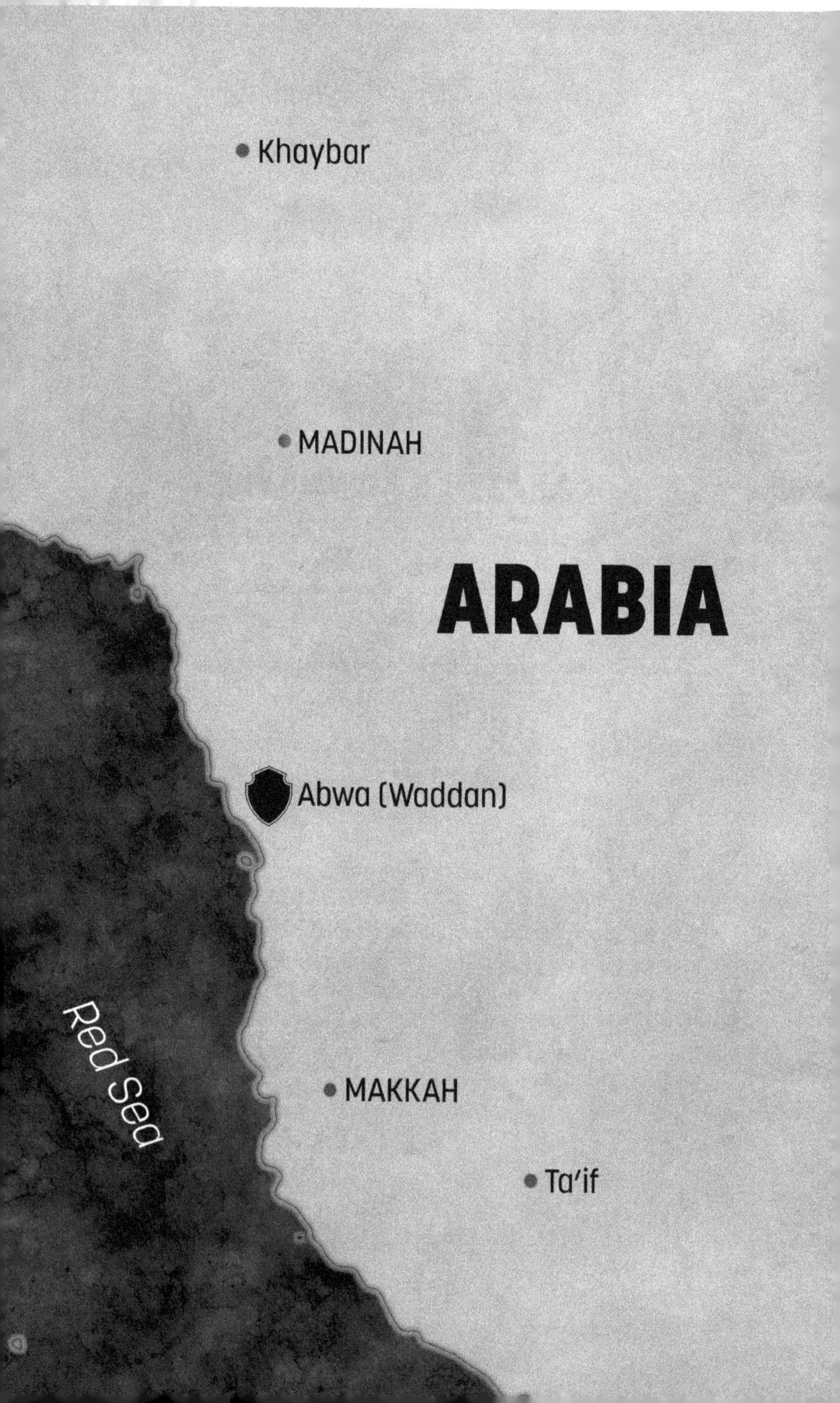
Khaybar
MADINAH
ARABIA
Abwa (Waddan)
Red Sea
MAKKAH
Ta'if

some authorities, the name belonged to a mountain situated there. It is mentioned in a general tradition that Prophet Muhammad's ﷺ mother, Amina, passed away in that area on her return journey to Madinah and was buried there.[10] During the beginning of the month of Safar in the second year of Hijrah, Prophet Muhammad ﷺ set out for battle with sixty[11] Muhajirūn.[12] He ﷺ set out on a military expedition to intercept the Qurayshi caravan, and the Banu Damrah tribe.[13] Upon his leaving, he appointed Sa'd bin Ubadah ؓ in charge of Madinah.[14]

With the battle flag held by Hamza ؓ, the Muslims marched forward for battle. However, on their arrival at Abwa they realised that the Qurayshi caravan had already departed. Matters were not left there; Prophet Muhammad ﷺ made a truce with the chief of Banu Damrah, namely, Mukhshi bin Amr, and a document to this effect was drawn up between them. Some of the conditions of this truce included the following:[15]

- Neither the Banu Damrah nor the Muslims would wage war against each other unless the Banu Damrah opposed the religion of Allah.
- The Banu Damrah would not betray the Muslims and would offer them aid when needed.
- The lives and the wealth of the Banu Damrah would be safe and secure.

After that, Prophet Muhammad ﷺ returned to Madinah within fifteen days without engaging in battle. There are a few accounts about the relations between tribes and kingdoms which help us understand each battle further. The Damrah were from the tribe of Kinanah, and the Bani Kinanah were the allies of the Quraysh in the wars of Fijār.[16] Their association is also evident during the significant event of the boycott, where the Quraysh urged boycott

---

10 *Qasas un-Nabiyeen*, 5/32 [Arabic], *Al-Rawd al-Unuf*, 3/34.
11 Some sources mention seventy Muhajirūn.
12 Muslims that migrated from Makkah to Madinah.
13 *Al-Rawd al-Unuf*, 3/33-34.
14 *Al-Rahīq ul-Makhtūm*, p.171.
15 Ibid.
16 *Al-Rahīq ul-Makhtūm*, p.54.

upon the Banu Hashim in connection with the missionary activities of Prophet Muhammad ﷺ, allowing their vicinity to be used for the pledge.[17]

17 Ibid p.95.

GHAZWAH BUWAT

The Muslims launched an attack against the trade caravan of the Quraysh heading towards Makkah.

Type:	Battle
Date:	Rabi' al-Awwal or Rabi' ath-Thani 2AH
Opposition:	Quraysh.
Prominent figures:	Umayyah bin Khalaf as leader
No. of Muslims:	200 Muhajirun
No. of Unbelievers:	Quraysh with 2500 camels and 100 tribesmen
Outcome:	No combat

Bawat, also pronounced Buwat, is the name of a mountain in the mountains of Juhaynah, close to Radwa (Yambu'),[18] approximately forty-eight miles from Madinah.[19]

With an army of just two hundred companions,[20] Prophet Muhammad ﷺ left Madinah for Buwat. This occurred when Prophet Muhammad ﷺ learned of a Qurayshi trade caravan en route to Makkah. The trade caravan comprised two thousand

---

18 *Fath ul-Bari, Kitāb ul-Maghazi* 7/349, *Al-Rawd al-Unuf* 3/42.
19 *Zarqāni* 1/456, *Fath ul-Bari, Kitaab ul-Maghazi* 7/349.
20 *Atlas as-Sīrah an-Nabawiyah* p.100 [Arabic version].

ARABIA

Khaybar •

Buwat

MADINAH •

Red Sea

• Badr

five hundred camels and one hundred tribesmen of the Quraysh[21] who were under the leadership of Ummayah bin Khalaf.

Leaving Uthman bin Maz'un ﷺ as a governor in Madinah,[22] Prophet Muhammad ﷺ departed for Buwat. Upon their arrival, they learned that the Qurayshi caravan had somehow slipped away. Hence, the Muslims returned to Madinah without engaging in any combat.

21 Ibid.
22 *Al-Rawd al-Unuf* 3/42, *Fath ul-Bari* 7/349.

GHAZWAH SAFWAN

Kurz bin Jabir al-Fihri launched a late-night attack. Before the departure for battle, Prophet Muhammad ﷺ appointed Zaid bin Harithah ؓ as his deputy in Madinah.

Other names:	Badr Al-Sughra
Type:	Battle
Date:	Rabi' al-Awwal 2AH
	10 days after the Prophet ﷺ
	returned from the battle of Ushayrah.
Opposition:	Quraysh tribe; their chief was Kurz bin
	Jabir ؓ who later accepted Islam.
No. of Muslims:	Unknown
No. of Unbelievers:	Unknown
Prominent figures:	Kurz bin Jabir Al-Fihri ؓ
Outcome:	No combat

Safwan is also referred to as Badr Sughra,[23] or 'the minor battle of Badr'. The incident occurred during Rabi' al-Awwal 2AH at a location very close to Badr,[24] hence why Safwan is often called Badr Sughra. In addition, during this battle Prophet Muhammad ﷺ traced back the trails of Kurz bin Jabir[25] from Safwan which led him to Badr.

23 *Al-Rawd al-Unuf* 3/46.
24 Ibid.
25 Ibid.

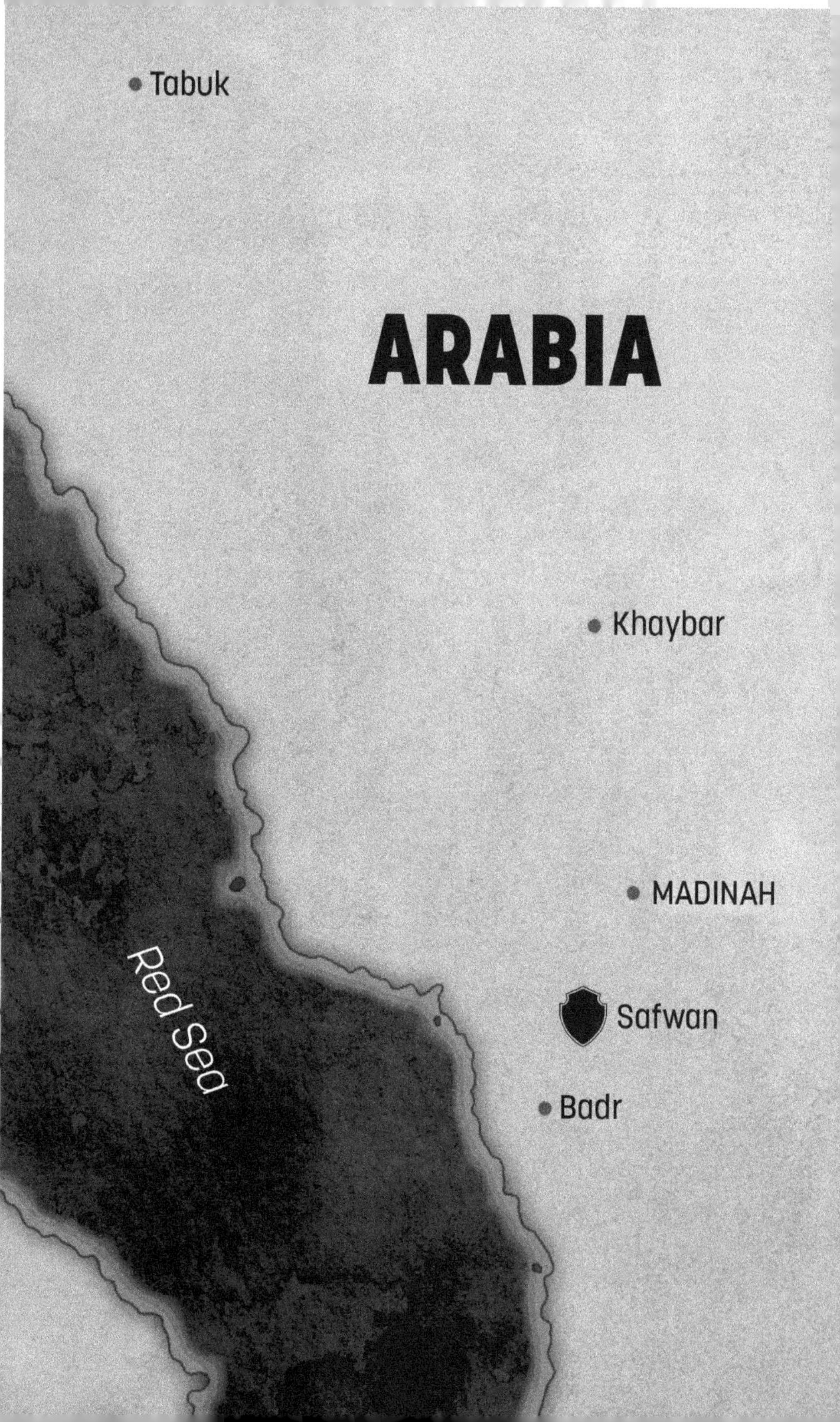
Tabuk
ARABIA
Khaybar
MADINAH
Red Sea
Safwan
Badr

Approximately ten days[26] after Prophet Muhammad ﷺ had returned to Madinah from the battle of Ushayrah, Kurz bin Jabir launched a late-night attack on the pastures of Madinah and he escaped with several camels and goats. As soon as Prophet Muhammad ﷺ received the news he set out in pursuit towards Safwan, leaving Zaid bin Harithah ؓ as the deputy of Madinah.[27]

When Prophet Muhammad ﷺ reached the location he realised that Kurz bin Jabir (one of the chiefs of a Qurayshi tribe who later accepted Islam) had somehow escaped from the area. Prophet Muhammad ﷺ remained in Madinah for the latter part of Jumada al-Akhirah, Rajab and Sha'ban. After his acceptance of Islam, Kurz bin Jabir was appointed as the Amir of a delegation that was despatched to the Uraniyyin[28] and later became a martyr at the conquest of Makkah.[29]

26 Ibid.
27 Ibid.
28 A group of people from Urainah came to Madinah and they discussed their discomfort about the climate change, hence the Prophet ﷺ gave them some camels from charity to drink its milk and urine as a cure.
29 Al-Isabah 5/434.

GHAZWAH BADR AL-KUBRA

Allah is the best of Planners; this battle, in which there were three battle flags, was not planned by the Quraysh nor by Prophet Muhammad ﷺ, but Allah Himself. When there is sincerity within an action, the aid of Allah is always there.

Type:	Battle
Date:	12th Ramadan/ 8th of Ramadan 2AH
Opposition:	Quraysh
No. of Muslims:	313-15 Muhajirun, 2 horses and 70 camels
Muslims martyred:	14
No. of Unbelievers:	1000 men with 700 camels
Unbelievers killed:	70
Prominent figures:	Abu Sufyan and his tribes
Outcome:	Muslims gained victory with the aid of Allah via the Angels

In the present day, Badr is recognised as a large town approximately 150 miles from Madinah. There are many opinions regarding the origin of its name. Some believe it is called Badr in honour of the founder of the area, either Badr bin Yakhlad bin Nadr bin Kinanah or Badr bin Harith. Others suggest it has been devoted to the name of a well there.[30]

---

30 *Al-Rawd al-Unuf* 3/54.

Khandaq •

• MADINAH

● Badr

ARABIA

Red Sea

• Hunayn

• MAKKAH

Ta'if •

The Battle of Badr is considered *Yawm ul-Furqān* (the Day of Distinguishing). It is the most decisive battle in the annals of Islam, marking the beginning of the defeat of the disbelievers and polytheists amongst the Quraysh, as mentioned in Surah Anfāl 'and We have sent down on Our servant on the Day of Furqān.'[31] During the early days of Ramadan in the year 2AH, Prophet Muhammad ﷺ received information that a valuable caravan was returning from Syria to Makkah, led by Abu Sufyan b. Harb, chief of the clan of Umayya.[32] The Muslims took this opportunity to attack the caravan in order to financially weaken the Quraysh. Abu Sufyan was alerted to the presence of Muslims when he witnessed camel droppings with Madinan seeds embedded in them. After that, he despatched Damdam Ghifari with the following message to Makkah: 'O people of Quraysh! The caravan, the caravan! Your wealth is with Abu Sufyan, but indeed Muhammad and his companions are heading towards it. I do not think [you will be able] to overtake it [caravan]. Help, help!'[33]

After despatching Damdam Ghifari to Makkah he alerted the Quraysh to the presence of the Muslims. Abu Sufyan, on his side, had sent a request to Makkah for a force to protect the caravan while it passed through the region, which was easily accessible from Madinah.[34] Abu Sufyan slipped away onto the coastal roads towards Makkah.[35] Despite the disapproval of some senior men and the withdrawal of the contingents from the clans of Banu Zuhra and Banu Adi,[36] Abu Jahl decided to go forward towards Badr and make a display of strength with a large and well-equipped army.

On the 12th of Ramadan 2AH, Prophet Muhammad ﷺ set out from Madinah with only 313–15 Mujahidīn, 2 horses, and 70 camels.[37] The Quraysh embarked on their journey with Abu Jahl

---

31 Surah Anfal: 41.
32 *Al-Rawd al-Unuf* 3/54.
33 Ibid, p.57.
34 Ibid.
35 Ibid.
36 Ibid.
37 Ibid, p.61.

as the leader of an army of 1,000 men and 700 camels.[38] They were accompanied by the archenemies of Prophet Muhammad ﷺ, being Ummayah bin Khalaf and Abu Jahl, whose ultimate goal was to demolish Islam once and for all. The Quraysh arrived first at Badr by the 17th, and then they chose the better ground.[39] On the morning of Saturday the 18th of Ramadan 2AH, two groups from the Quraysh took up positions for battle.[40] Prophet Muhammad ﷺ positioned the Muslims and returned to his shelter.[41] Soon after, the Quraysh took their positions for battle. Prophet Muhammad ﷺ proceeded to the plains of Badr with his high-spirited companions and *tawakkul* (trust) in Allah.

When Prophet Muhammad ﷺ laid eyes on the large, well-equipped Qurayshi army, he submitted before Allah Ta'ala:

اللهمّ هذه قريش قد أقبلت بخيلائها ونخرها تحادّك وتكذّب رسولك

اللهمّ فنصرك الذي وعدتني اللهمّ أحنهم الغداة

O Allah, here are the Quraysh who are drawing near with their vanity and haughtiness to oppose and to falsify your messenger ﷺ. O Allah, I seek your help that which you promised. O Allah, destroy them by morning.[42]

He raised his hands to the sky until the cloak fell from his shoulders. Abu Bakr ؓ consoled and comforted him. After that, Prophet Muhammad ﷺ arranged the ranks of the Muslims in proper fighting formation. Utbah bin Rabi'ah, his brother Shaybah ibn Rabi'ah and his son Al-Walīd stepped forward from the Quraysh army to fight. When they came forward, they asked for the same from the opposing party, as was the custom. When three youths from the Ansār[43] came forward they asked for someone

38 Ibid.
39 Ibid, pp.70-1.
40 *Qasas un Nabiyeen*, 5/142-143.
41 Ibid p.142-3.
42 *Al-Rawd al-Unuf* 3/72.
43 Muslims in Madinah who are known as the 'helpers.'

of their equal. Thereafter, Prophet Muhammad ﷺ sent ahead Ubayda bin Al-Harith ؓ, Hamza ؓ and Ali ؓ. As they exchanged blows with Utbah bin Rabi'ah, Shaybah bin Rabi'ah and Al-Walīd, resulting in their deaths, Ali ؓ and Hamza ؓ carried back Ubayda ؓ, who was wounded and later passed away as a martyr.[44]

War broke out, swords collided and arrows were shot. On that day the faith of the Muslims was heightened, their hearts burned with the love of Allah and their vision was paradise. This is seen in the two valiant brothers who fought courageously beside one another for the sake of Allah. Abdur Rahman bin Awf ؓ narrates this interesting story of the 'two young boys'.[45] He recalls how on the day of Badr when he was positioned in his row, he looked towards his left and right to find two Ansāri boys. One called out saying: 'O uncle, do you know Abu Jahl?' Abdur Rahman bin Awf ؓ replied: 'Yes, what do you want from him?' Upon which he replied, 'I have heard that he troubles Prophet Muhammad ﷺ. By Him in whose hands my life is, if I see him I will not stop fighting him until death do us part! I have made an oath with Allah that if I see him, I will kill him or die before him.' The other boy then made the same statement.

44 Ibid, p.75.
45 Ibn Hajr: Mua'z and Mua'wizz, sons of Afrah.

Abdur Rahman bin Awf ﷺ later proclaimed that when he saw Abu Jahl amongst the people he directed the boys to him. They marched towards him and struck him with their swords until they killed him, after which they went to inform Prophet Muhammad ﷺ.[46] When Abu Jahl was killed and thereafter presented by Abdullah bin Masood ﷺ, Prophet Muhammad ﷺ first glorified Allah and then remarked that 'this Abu Jahl was the Pharaoh of this community.'[47]

During this same battle, the two great archenemies of Prophet Muhammad ﷺ were erased, one being Abu Jahl and the other Ummayah ibn Khalaf and his son. Whilst waging an intense battle against the enemy, Allah Ta'ala sent down one thousand, then three thousand and finally five thousand angels to aid the Muslims.[48] With the aid of Allah and rejuvenated faith, the Muslims gained victory. Following this, to share the good news with the others, Prophet Muhammad ﷺ despatched his messengers to Madinah. He sent Abdullah bin Rawahah ﷺ towards the upper regions and Zaid bin Harithah towards the lower regions of Madinah. Allah revealed the following verse after Badr, concerning the battle:

$$ قَدْ كَانَ لَكُمْ آيَةٌ فِي فِئَتَيْنِ الْتَقَتَا ۖ فِئَةٌ تُقَاتِلُ فِي سَبِيلِ اللَّهِ وَأُخْرَىٰ كَافِرَةٌ يَرَوْنَهُم مِّثْلَيْهِمْ رَأْيَ الْعَيْنِ ۚ وَاللَّهُ يُؤَيِّدُ بِنَصْرِهِ مَن يَشَاءُ ۗ إِنَّ فِي ذَٰلِكَ لَعِبْرَةً لِّأُولِي الْأَبْصَارِ $$

Indeed there already was for you a sign from the two parties that met, [in it] one fighting in the path of Allah and the other of disbelievers. They saw them [to be] twice their number with their eyesight. But Allah supports with His help whoever He wills. Indeed, in that is a lesson for those who have eyes.[49]

---

46 *Al-Rawd al-Unuf* 3/88, *Sahih Bukhari* 3141.
47 *Al-Rahīq ul-Makhtūm* p.191.
48 *Tafsir Baydawi* 1/183.
49 Surah Al-Imran: 13.

GHAZWAH AL-USHAYRAH

Ushayrah is close to Yambu'. The Muslims left to attack a Qurayshi caravan. However, when they arrived the caravan had already left. Prophet Muhammad ﷺ appointed Abu Salamah bin Abdul Asad ؓ as his vice-regent in Madinah.

Type:	Expedition
Date:	Jumada al-Ula 2AH
Opposition:	Quraysh
No. of Muslims::	200 Muhajirun with 30 camels which the companions took turns riding.
No. of Unbelievers:	Unknown
Outcome:	A peace treaty was made.

Ushayrah is a village in the Madinan region near Yambu'. Today, the distance between Ushayrah and Yambu' is approximately 371km/230miles.[50] It is considered a rather tiresome and difficult journey on foot from Madinah, approximately 20 miles away.[51]

During Jumada al-Ula in the second year of Hijrah, Prophet Muhammad ﷺ, with the company of two hundred companions, marched towards an area to the west of Saudi Arabia named Ushayrah. They shared thirty or so camels as a means of transport to reach their destination and cavalry for any forthcoming battles.

50 https://saudi-arabia.places-in-the-world.com/100662-distances-from-ushayrah-to-the-largest-places-in-saudi-arabia.html?page=1
51 *Al-Rawd al-Unuf* 3/44.

ARABIA

Khaybar

Uhud
MADINAH

Ushayrah

MAKKAH
Hudaybiyah

Red Sea

NUBIA

When the Muslims arrived at their intended location, Prophet Muhammad ﷺ could not locate the Qurayshi trade caravan he came to pursue. As a result, he spent the remaining days of Jumada al-Ula and a few days of Jumada al-Akhirah at the location.

During his stay, he made a peace treaty with the Banu Mudlij without engaging in any physical combat. Here is a sample of what the peace treaty consisted of:

بسم الله الرحمن الرحيم، هذا كتاب من محمد رسول الله لبني ضمرة بأنهم آمنون على أموالهم وأنفسهم، وأن النصرة على من رامهم إلا أن يحاربوا في دين الله ما بل بحر صوفة والمقصود للأبد-، وأن محمد رسول الله إذا دعاهم لنصره أجابوه، عليهم بذلك ذمة الله وذمة رسوله ولهم النصر على من بر منهم واتقى

In the name of Allah the Most Gracious the Most Merciful. This agreement is from Muhammad the Messenger of Allah to the Banu Damrah. Indeed, that themselves and their wealth are safe and they will be helped against those who attack them in consideration that they do not engage in combat with the religion of Allah. [This agreement will be intact] until the sea of Sufah does not dry. And when Prophet Muhammad ﷺ calls upon them to help they shall respond to him [with their aid]. This is the pledge of Allah and His Messenger over them. Help is for those who are devoted and God-fearing.[52]

Since the expedition came to an end and no battle was waged Prophet Muhammad ﷺ left for Madinah, where he appointed Abdul-Asad ﷺ as his vice-regent.

52 *Zarqānī* 2/236.

GHAZWAH AL-QAYNUQA

The Banu Qaynuqa broke the pact with Prophet Muhammad ﷺ. On Saturday the 15th or 16th of Shawwal, Prophet Muhammad ﷺ went to their marketplace and invited them to Islam. They denied and mocked Prophet Muhammad ﷺ; thereafter verse 13 of Surah Al-Imran was revealed.

Type:	Expedition
Date:	Saturday 15th Shawwal 2AH
Opposition:	Banu Qaynuqa (Jews)
No. of Muslims:	Unknown
No. of Unbelievers:	Unknown
Outcome:	Muslims gained victory

The Banu Qaynuqa were one of the three prominent Jewish tribes present in Yathrib, now commonly known as Madinah. Unlike the other Jewish tribes, they did not possess agricultural lands but they did have strong fortresses and markets. They earned their living through trade and craftsmanship and were considered to be courageous and skilful people. Although being of the Jewish faith, they were considered to be amongst the kinsfolk of Abdullah bin Salam. Madinah consisted of three prominent Jewish tribes: the Banu Nadir, the Banu Qaynuqa and the Banu Qurayzah. Amongst the three tribes, the first to violate the treaty drawn up by Prophet Muhammad ﷺ upon his entry to Madinah

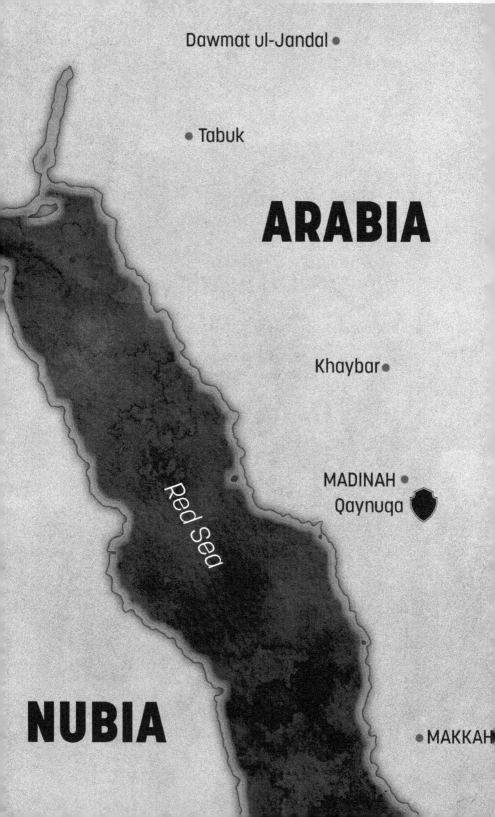

were the Banu Qaynuqa. The treaty highlighted that these three tribes would refrain from waging war against Prophet Muhammad's 🕌 will nor support the Prophet's enemies in doing so.

The incident which aggravated the conflict between the Muslims and the Banu Qaynuqa was when a Muslim woman proceeded to the market of Banu Qaynuqa to sell her goods. They attempted to reveal her face, but upon her refusal, the jeweller tied a corner of her garment to her back when she sat down. This resulted in the exposure of her *awrah*[53] upon standing. They laughed at her and she was humiliated. When she called for help, a fellow Muslim approached the Jewish jeweller and killed him. At that instant, a man from the Banu Qaynuqa approached the Muslim and killed him.[54] Havoc broke out as the family of the Muslim cried for help. The news reached Prophet Muhammad 🕌 and he proceeded towards the market to speak to the Banu Qaynuqa on Saturday the 15th or 16th Shawwal. Prophet Muhammad 🕌 gathered the tribe together and addressed them, saying:

يا معشر اليهود، احذروا من الله عزّ وجلّ مثل ما نزل بقريش من النقمة، وأسلموا فإنكم قد عرفتم أني نبي مرسل، تجدون ذلك في كتابكم وفي عهد الله إليكم

O assembly of Jews! Be warned of a punishment from Allah like the punishment that struck the Quraysh. Accept Islam, for you know that I am a true Messenger of Allah. You find this in your books and Allah has taken an oath regarding this from you.[55]

The reason for the intensity of Prophet Muhammad 🕌's statement was the breaching of the law by the Banu Qaynuqa. This pact was commissioned after Prophet Muhammad 🕌 migrated to Madinah. The peace accord was to:

---

53 Intimate parts of a man and woman's body that must be covered.
54 *Al-Rawd al-Unuf* 3/241.
55 Ibid p.240.

- Refrain from waging war against the Muslims
- Refrain from assisting the enemies of Islam

As previously mentioned, the Banu Qaynuqa were not fearful of breaking the law, even more so after Prophet Muhammad ﷺ made his statement in the market of Madinah. The Jews responded by saying: 'O Muhammad, did you think of us to be your nation? Do not be fooled by your victory over a nation that is not knowledgeable about war, as you had an advantage over them! Indeed, by Allah, if you had fought against us only then would you come to know that we are the true definition of men.'[56] Appointing Abu Lubabah bin Abul-Munzir as his representative in Madinah, Prophet Muhammad ﷺ set out towards the locality of Banu Qaynuqa. When the Banu Qaynuqa came to know of Prophet Muhammad's ﷺ arrival they took refuge in one of their fortresses and sealed the entrance. Prophet Muhammad ﷺ laid siege to the fort for approximately fifteen days from the fifteenth of Shawwal to the first of Dhul-Qa'dah. Due to the constrained circumstances they found themselves in, the Banu Qaynuqa surrendered and in return were banished from Madinah. Goods from the opposition were taken as booty and after Badr this was the first *khums* (one-fifth) where Prophet Muhammad ﷺ attained one fifth for himself and his family and thereafter distributed the remaining four fifths amongst the Mujahidīn.

GHAZWAH AL-SAWĪQ

A campaign triggered by a member of Abu Sufyan's army killing an Ansari and a labourer. Abu Sufyan and his army already departed the area before a fight could ensue.

Type:	Campaign
Date:	5th Dhul-Hijjah 2AH
Opposition:	Makkans
No. of Muslims:	200 Muhajirun and Ansar
Prominent figures:	Abu Sufyan
No. of Unbelievers	200 men
Outcome:	Abu Sufyan and his army had already departed before a fight could happen.

Sawīq[57] was the name given to this campaign after Abu Sufyan bin Harb and his army left behind bags of *sawīq* (porridge) to lessen their burden while fleeing from the locality.[58] During the fifth of Dhul-Hijjah 2AH whilst returning from Badr, Abu Sufyan bin Harb vowed to not take a ritual bath and remain in a state of *janābah* (ritual impurity) until he waged a war against Prophet Muhammad ﷺ. Keeping to his word, he set out with an army of two hundred mounted men towards the direction of Madinah. He

57 Crushed wheat flavoured with ghee.
58 *Atlas Sīrah tun Nabawiyyah* p. 112.

• Khaybar

ARABIA

 Sawiq

Khandaq •

• MADINAH

Red Sea

Badr •

stopped to pay a visit to an old friend named Huyayy bin Akhtab who was afraid to let him into his home. He later turned his attention towards Salman bin Miksham, a chief of the Banu Nadir, who gave him an insight into the affairs of Madinah.[59] Thereafter, upon reaching an area called Uraid approximately three miles before Madinah, Abu Sufyan bin Harb and his troop cunningly crept into a date orchard whilst two Ansāri labourers[60] were cultivating the land. After killing the pair he set fire to a few trees in the area. Satisfied that he had fulfilled his vow, he returned to Makkah.[61]

Soon after, word reached Prophet Muhammad ﷺ and he set out on Sunday 5th Dhul-Hijjah 2AH accompanied by two hundred Muhajirūn and Ansār[62] in pursuit of Abu Sufyan bin Harb. However, upon their arrival they realised that Abu Sufyan bin Harb and his troop had long since departed the vicinity. To lessen their load, the delegation had left behind bags of *sawīq*, hence the name of the campaign.

---

59 *Zarqāni* 2/354.
60 *Al-Rawd al-Unuf* 2/237.
61 Ibid.
62 *Zarqāni* 2/353-55.

35

GHAZWAH QARQARAH TUL KUDR

A battle initiated because Prophet Muhammad ﷺ heard that the Sulaim and Ghatafan forces were coming to attack the Muslims.

Type:	Expedition
Date:	Shawwal-Half of Muharram 2AH
Opposition:	Sulaim and Ghatafan forces
No. of Muslims:	200 men
No. of Unbelievers	They dispersed upon hearing Prophet Muhammad's ﷺ arrival.
Outcome:	After Prophet Muhammad ﷺ stayed in the springs of Kudr for three days, he returned without engaging in any combat.

Kudr is a spring from the many springs of Bani Sulaim, located in Najd on the eastern side between Makkah and Syria.[63] Allama Suhayli has defined it as follows: 'Qarqarah is a smooth land. Al-Kudr is a brown colour that is found on a bird. [It can be] specifically [found] on buildings in the cities of Suwaydarah[64] and al-Hanakiyah.[65] If you go to Qasim it is situated on the right;

---

63 *Al-Rahīq ul-Makhtūm* p.202.
64 By walking 70.4km from Madinah.
65 By walking 117km from Madinah.

ARABIA

MADINAH •

Kudr

Safwan •

Red Sea

• Waddan

there is a wide field which stretches to the fields of Bani Sulaim and presently it is known as Mahd uz-Zahab.'[66]

During the beginning of the month of Shawwal, as the Muslims returned exhausted from the Battle of Badr, Prophet Muhammad ﷺ was informed of a possible threat from the Bani Sulaim and Ghatafan tribes.[67] Upon receiving this news Prophet Muhammad ﷺ set out with an army of two hundred men.[68] When they arrived they found that the tribes of Bani Sulaim and Ghatafan[69] had already dispersed on hearing about the arrival of the Muslims.

After spending three days at the location with no sign of the opposition, Prophet Muhammad ﷺ returned to Madinah without engaging in any combat.[70]

66 *Al-Rawd al-Unuf* 3/236.
67 *Al-Raheeq-ul-Makhtoom* p.202.
68 *Zarqāni* 2/345.
69 *Al-Rawd al-Unuf* 3/236, *Atlas Sīrah Nabawiyyah* p.112.
70 *Al-Rawd al-Unuf* 3/236.

GHAZWAH AL-GHATAFAN

Banu Tha'labah and Banu Maharib were assembling in Najd with the intention to plunder the surrounding areas of Madinah. Prophet Muhammad ﷺ appointed Uthman ibn Affan ﷺ as the representative in Madinah. During this journey, a heavy rain left Prophet Muhammad ﷺ and the Companions drenched. Prophet Muhammad ﷺ and the Companions hung their clothes on a tree and lay down to rest, when a Bedouin saw them and informed their commander Da'thur.

Type:	Campaign
Other names:	Campaign of Anmar and Zu Amar
Date:	Muharram 3AH,
	12th Rabi' al-Awwal 3AH
Opposition:	Banu Tha'labah and Banu Maharib
No. of Muslims:	450 Companions
No. of Unbelievers:	Unknown
Prominent figures:	Da'thur
Outcome:	No combat

The Bani Ghatafan were one of the tribes of Madinah. This campaign is also known as Anmar or Zu Amar and was in the vicinity of an-Nukhayl, Najd, in the lands of Bani Ghatafan.[71] After returning from Sawīq, Prophet Muhammad ﷺ spent the remaining days of Dhul-Hijjah in Madinah. During this period, Prophet

71 Ibid p.239.

ARABIA

Ghatafan
(Zu Amar)

Uhud •

• MADINAH

Ushayrah •

Red Sea

Muhammad ﷺ learned that two subdivisions of the Banu Ghatafan, namely, the Banu Maharib and the Banu Tha'labah, under the command of Da'thur bin Harith al-Maharibi, were assembling in an area of Najd to attack the surrounding areas of Madinah.[72]

Leaving Uthman bin Affan ؓ as his representative in Madinah,[73] Prophet Muhammad ﷺ set out with four hundred and fifty companions in the month of Muharram. Some have suggested that this was on the 12th of Rabi' al-Awwal 3AH. When the Banu Ghatafan sensed the presence of Prophet Muhammad ﷺ, they dispersed into the mountains. The companions managed to locate one member of the Banu Tha'labah named Hiban. He was later brought before Prophet Muhammad ﷺ and was invited to Islam, which he accepted. Prophet Muhammad ﷺ assigned him to Bilal ؓ to learn the rulings of Shariah from him. Thereafter, the Prophet Muhammad spent ﷺ the entire month of Safar[74] in the locality of Ghatafan. He did not witness, nor was he confronted by any of the opposition. Without engaging in any physical combat, Prophet Muhammad ﷺ returned to Madinah in Rabi' al-Awwal.[75]

At one point during their journey, heavy rainfall left Prophet Muhammad ﷺ and his companions drenched, which led them to seek shelter under a tree, leaving their clothes hanging on a nearby tree to dry. As Prophet Muhammad ﷺ lay down to rest, a bedouin from the locality became aware of his presence. He alerted his commander Da'thur by saying: 'Prophet Muhammad ﷺ is by himself and there is no one with him' suggesting the commander should take this golden opportunity to kill Prophet Muhammad ﷺ.

Da'thur valiantly held his sword and approached Prophet Muhammad ﷺ. He focused the sharp sword upon the head of Prophet Muhammad ﷺ exclaiming: 'O Muhammad! Tell me who will save you from my sword today?' Prophet Muhammad ﷺ

---

72 *Zarqānī* 2/379.
73 *Al-Rawd al-Unuf* 3/239.
74 This will be the view of those who are of the opinion that Prophet Muhammad ﷺ set out for the campaign in Muharram and not Rabi' al-Awwal.
75 Ibid.

responded composedly, 'Allah.' Just as he uttered this, by the command of Allah, Jibrīl ﷺ struck Da'thur with a severe blow to his chest, resulting in his sword flying out of his hand.

Prophet Muhammad ﷺ retrieved the sword and posed the same question to Da'thur, 'Now tell me, who will save you from my sword?'[76] Da'thur replied, 'Nobody will save me from you.' With the kalimah on his lips he left the presence of Prophet Muhammad ﷺ, exclaiming that neither he nor his people would wage war against him.

When he returned to his people, they were perplexed by his actions and asked him what the matter was. He recalled his incident with Prophet Muhammad ﷺ and the miraculous experience with Jibrīl ﷺ. It has been stated that he envisioned a tall white man strike him on his chest and knew that this could not be anyone other than an angel. Thus he accepted Islam and invited his people to do so accordingly. Allah, the Most High, mentions this remarkable incident in the Holy Qur'an:

$$\text{يَا أَيُّهَا الَّذِينَ آمَنُوا اذْكُرُوا نِعْمَتَ اللَّهِ عَلَيْكُمْ إِذْ هَمَّ قَوْمٌ أَن يَبْسُطُوا إِلَيْكُمْ}$$

$$\text{أَيْدِيَهُمْ فَكَفَّ أَيْدِيَهُمْ عَنكُمْ وَاتَّقُوا اللَّهَ وَعَلَى اللَّهِ فَلْيَتَوَكَّلِ الْمُؤْمِنُونَ}^{77}$$

O you who believe, remember the blessings Allah has bestowed
upon you when a nation was interested that they extend upon
you their hands [in aggression] so He withheld their hands from
you; and fear Allah. And let the believers rely upon Allah.

---

76 *Zarqāni* 2/381.
77 Surah Maidah:11.

GHAZWAH AL-BUHRAN

*The Banu Sulaim were amassing against the Muslims, but dispersed
before Prophet Muhammad ﷺ came with his companions.*

Type:	Expedition
Other names:	Banu Sulaim
Date:	Rabi' al-Akhir,
	2nd Jumada al-Ula 3AH
Opposition:	Banu Sulaim
No. of Muslims:	300 Companions
No. of Unbelievers:	Unknown
Outcome:	No combat; the Bani Sulaim
	dispersed before Prophet Muhammad
	ﷺ came with his companions.

Buhran, in the vicinity of al-Fur, is a valley from the valleys of
Hijaz, 150 km towards the south of Madinah.[78] It is said that this
was one of the first villages that Hajar ﵍ and Isma'il ﵍ passed
on their journey to Makkah.[79]

After returning from the campaign of Ghatafan, Prophet Muhammad ﷺ spent the rest of Rabi' al-Awwal in Madinah. During
the month of Rabi' ath-Thani, Prophet Muhammad ﷺ received
news that the Bani Sulaim were mobilising against the Muslims

78 *Al-Rawd al-Unuf* 3/239.
79 *Zarqāni* 2/382.

Badr

Buhran

ARABIA

MAKKAH

Hudaybiyah

Ta'if

in a locality called Buhran. On hearing of their plan, Prophet Muhammad ﷺ arranged for three hundred companions to accompany him there.[80]

Leaving Abdullah bin Umm Maktum ؓ as his representative in Madinah, Prophet Muhammad ﷺ set off with the companions towards Buhran.[81] Having heard speculations of Prophet Muhammad's ﷺ arrival, the Banu Buhran dispersed. Without engaging in battle, Prophet Muhammad ﷺ returned to Madinah. There is a difference of opinion regarding how long Prophet Muhammad ﷺ resided in Buhran. Some say it was ten nights whilst Ibn Sa'd mentions that Prophet Muhammad ﷺ remained there until the 16th of Jumada al-Ula.[82]

---

80 Ibid.
81 Ibid.
82 Ibid, p.383.

GHAZWAH UHUD

Those who are disobedient to Allah will be accountable for it. Abu Sufyan decided that the money left from the caravan of Badr was to be used in a fight against Prophet Muhammad ﷺ. This battle taught the Muslims to be obedient towards Prophet Muhammad ﷺ. Allah tests his servants in both good and bad times, in that which they like and dislike, in victory and defeat. It teaches us to show obedience to Allah regardless of the situation.

Type:	Battle
Date:	6th Shawwal 3AH
Opposition:	Quraysh
No. of Muslims:	1000 men at first, then 700
Muslims martyred:	70
No. of Unbelievers:	3000 men, 700 camels, 700 armour-clad warriors, 200 horses and 300 camels.
Unbelievers killed:	23-37
Prominent figures:	Abu Sufyan and Abu Jahl
Outcome:	Non-Muslims

Uhud is derived from the word *wahid* or *ahad*, which means single or unique. This famous mountain of Madinah is red in colour without large rock boulders. It is considered the head of all mountains, and the distance between it and Madinah is approximately two miles from the northern side. To further establish its

• Khaybar

ARABIA

 Uhud

• MADINAH

Red Sea

• Badr

distinctiveness from the rest of the mountains, it is narrated by Anas bin Malik ﷺ that Prophet Muhammad ﷺ said: 'This is a mountain that loves us and is loved by us. O Allah! Ibrahim ﷺ made Makkah sacred, and I make [the area] in between these two mountains sacred.'[83] Hence, it was given the name Uhud.[84]

As the Quraysh returned home exhausted and defeated, they discovered that the trade caravan that escaped with Abu Sufyan was safely secured in Dar un-Nadwah. The Quraysh had suffered humiliation from the defeat at Badr. Those who had lost their loved ones were seeking revenge, consumed by anger and hatred. With emotions running high, Abu Sufyan, Abdullah bin Rabi'ah, Ikrimah bin Abi Jahl, Harith bin Hisham, Huwayth bin Abdul Uzza, Safwan bin Ummayah and other prominent leading figures gathered for a special meeting.[85] They all proposed to gather the profit from the trade caravan in Dar un-Nadwah and spend it to purchase equipment in preparation for war against Prophet Muhammad ﷺ. They saw this as a means to settle old scores with the Muslims, who had killed their family members in Badr. All attendants approved of the proposal and amassed an amount of fifty thousand dinars and a thousand camels for this purpose. At this point Allah revealed the following verse:[86]

$$إِنَّ الَّذِينَ كَفَرُوا يُنفِقُونَ أَمْوَالَهُمْ لِيَصُدُّوا عَن سَبِيلِ اللَّهِ ۚ فَسَيُنفِقُونَهَا ثُمَّ تَكُونُ عَلَيْهِمْ حَسْرَةً ثُمَّ يُغْلَبُونَ ۗ وَالَّذِينَ كَفَرُوا إِلَىٰ جَهَنَّمَ يُحْشَرُونَ$$ [87]

Indeed, those who disbelieve spend their money to divert [people] from the path of Allah. So they will spend it and it will become a regret for them and then they will be defeated. And those who have disbelieved shall be gathered in Hell.

83 *Sahih Bukhari* 3367.
84 *Al-Rawd al-Unuf* 3/258.
85 Ibid p.259.
86 Ibid, *Zarqāni* 2/391.
87 Surah Anfal, 36.

To uplift their morale and inspire hope, the Quraysh elected a few women to accompany them in their parade to war.[88] Their duty was to recite poems and build the warriors' courage whilst humiliating those who deserted them. The Quraysh despatched messengers with invitations to join them in war. They were able to gather an army of three thousand men, seven hundred of whom were well-armed, two hundred horses, three thousand camels, and fifteen women.[89] On the fifth of Shawwal, this well-equipped army set out from Makkah with Abu Sufyan as their chief commander.

Prophet Muhammad ﷺ was notified of Abu Sufyan's intentions by a messenger from the Banu Ghifār sent by Abbas ﷺ, who insisted the message reach Prophet Muhammad ﷺ within three days.[90] As soon as the message reached Prophet Muhammad ﷺ he wasted no time but immediately sent Anas ﷺ and Munis ﷺ to gather intelligence about the Quraysh and their whereabouts. They returned to inform that the Quraysh were drawing near Madinah and had settled in the middle of a valley before Uhud in the direction of Madinah. Prophet Muhammad ﷺ sent them out again to deduce the number of their army. Upon returning, they gave Prophet Muhammad ﷺ an exact estimation of Abu Sufyan's warriors and cavalry.

As the night closed in, Sa'd bin Mu'az ﷺ, Usaid bin Hudair ﷺ, and Sa'd bin Ubadah ﷺ spent the hours on night watch in Masjid un-Nabawi (The Prophet's ﷺ Mosque) whilst other guards were dispersed around the town.[91] The next morning, Prophet Muhammad ﷺ consulted with the companions and invited them to share their views and suggestions. There was a disagreement regarding strategies. The senior companions deemed it wise to engage with the enemy whilst taking refuge within the territories of Madinah. However, the junior companions, who were unable to take part at Badr, were fully determined to take the battle to the enemy, outside of Madinah. A trait of a great leader is one who consults

88 *Al-Rawd al-Unuf* 3/261.
89 *Zarqāni* 2/400.
90 Ibid p.392.
91 *Al-Rahīq ul-Makhtūm* p.215.

his companions and then makes the final decision. Likewise, after hearing the objections and views of his companions, Prophet Muhammad ﷺ addressed them by describing a dream of his.

> Indeed I saw a dream and I swear by Allah it is good. I saw a cow and I saw it being slaughtered by a blunt knife. And I saw that I entered my hand into strong armour. So I give preference to [staying in] Madinah.

Ibn Hisham notes that Prophet Muhammad ﷺ later interpreted the cow being slaughtered as indicating that 'some of my companions will attain martyrdom, and as for the dent in the knife, that I will lose a family member of mine [in battle].'[92] The issue was raised to Abdullah bin Ubayy, the leader of the hypocrites, who was experienced in such matters. He informed the Muslims by recalling the fact that all the battles the Madinans were successful in were due to them staying within the boundaries of the city. He reminded them that when the battle was taken out of Madinah it resulted in catastrophe for the Madinans.

After the Friday congregational prayer, Prophet Muhammad ﷺ revealed his final verdict. In the sermon, he acknowledged the devotion and the enthusiasm of the companions to meet Allah and to attain Paradise. He understood that it was their sincerity that sparked within them the determination and eagerness to fight the battle outside of Madinah. The word spread and the Muslims were instructed by Prophet Muhammad ﷺ to prepare for battle. The following day after Asr prayer, as the preparations started, Prophet Muhammad ﷺ went into his room to don his armour. He was accompanied by two of his close companions, Abu Bakr ؓ and Umar ؓ.[93] On Friday the eleventh of Shawwal 3AH[94] after Asr prayer, Prophet Muhammad ﷺ left Madinah with an army of a thousand men. He mounted his horse, accompanied by Sa'd bin Mu'az ؓ whilst Sa'd bin Ubadah marched ahead. Upon reaching the outskirts of Madinah, namely, a place called Shaykhayn, Prophet Muhammad ﷺ inspected his army and sent

92 *Al-Rawd al-Unuf* 3/262, *Zarqānī* 2/392-393.
93 *Al-Rahīq ul-Makhtūm* p.216.
94 *Zarqānī* 2/389.

warriors who were too young home.[95] As the Muslims drew closer to Uhud, Abdullah bin Ubayy and three hundred other men decided to retract from the battle and return to Madinah. His justification was: 'You disregarded my request. Why should we get ourselves killed?'[96] Upon this act of disloyalty, the following verse was revealed:

$$وَلِيَعْلَمَ الَّذِينَ نَافَقُوا ۚ وَقِيلَ لَهُمْ تَعَالَوْا قَاتِلُوا فِي سَبِيلِ اللَّهِ أَوِ ادْفَعُوا ۖ قَالُوا لَوْ نَعْلَمُ قِتَالًا لَّاتَّبَعْنَاكُمْ ۗ هُمْ لِلْكُفْرِ يَوْمَئِذٍ أَقْرَبُ مِنْهُمْ لِلْإِيمَانِ ۚ يَقُولُونَ بِأَفْوَاهِهِم مَّا لَيْسَ فِي قُلُوبِهِمْ ۗ وَاللَّهُ أَعْلَمُ بِمَا يَكْتُمُونَ$$

And to know those who are hypocrites, it was said to them 'Come and fight in the cause of Allah or defend' and they said, 'If we had known that you were fighting then we would have followed you.' They were closer to disbelief than faith on that day, saying with their mouths that which was not in their hearts. Allah is all-Knowing of what they conceal.[97]

With Abdullah bin Ubayy retreating with his army, the Muslim army now consisted of only seven hundred men of which one hundred were equipped. After taking refuge in Shaykhayn for a short period, towards the latter part of the night Prophet Muhammad ﷺ set off with his army.[98] As the journey commenced, the time for Fajr prayer came upon them. Bilal ؓ announced the call to prayer and the Muslims prayed their salah in congregation with Prophet Muhammad ﷺ as their imam.

Battles are won by strategy, and this one was no different. Fifty archers were placed at the back of Mount Uhud with Abdullah bin Jubair ؓ[99] as their leader, to foresee any attack of the Quraysh from that direction.[100] The archers were given clear

95 *Al-Rahīq ul-Makhtūm* p.217.
96 *Al-Rawd al-Unuf* 3/263.
97 Surah Imran:167.
98 *Al-Rahīq ul-Makhtūm* p.217.
99 Ibid p.219.
100 Ibid p.266.

and distinct instructions by Prophet Muhammad ﷺ to 'not leave their position' whatever the circumstance. It has been narrated by Al-Bara bin Azib ؓ that Prophet Muhammad ﷺ said:

إِنْ رَأَيْتُمُونَا تَخْطَفُنَا الطَّيْرُ، فَلَا تَبْرَحُوا مَكَانَكُمْ هَذَا حَتَّى أُرْسِلَ إِلَيْكُمْ، وَإِنْ رَأَيْتُمُونَا هَزَمْنَا الْقَوْمَ وَأَوْطَأْنَاهُمْ فَلَا تَبْرَحُوا حَتَّى أُرْسِلَ إِلَيْكُمْ

Even if you see birds grabbing us, do not leave your posts until I send for you; even if you see that we have defeated the group of people and we have trampled over them, [even then] do not leave your post until I call for you.[101]

The army of the Quraysh arrived at Uhud on Wednesday and camped at the lowest part of Mount Uhud. They brought a superior army of three thousand men, seven hundred armoured warriors, two hundred horses, and three thousand camels.[102] With the troops settled, chosen warriors were assigned to their designated roles. Khalid bin Walīd ؓ was chosen as the commander of the right flank whilst Ikrimah bin Abi Jahl ؓ[103] was appointed as the left, leaving Safwan bin Umayyah ؓ as the commander of the infantry and Abdullah bin Rabi'ah ؓ as the commander of the archers. As both parties drew their battle lines, Abu Dujānah ؓ was offered the sword of Prophet Muhammad ﷺ in aspiration to fulfil its due right.[104] He used to wear a red band across his head which symbolised his readiness to fight.[105] It is said that when Prophet Muhammad ﷺ offered his sword before the people and asked, 'Who will fulfil the right of this sword?', no one volunteered until Abu Dujānah, Simāk bin Kharashah and Akhu bin Sa'adah stood up. They asked 'What is its right, O Muhammad?' He ﷺ replied: 'To strike the enemies with it until it becomes bent [breaks].' Someone said, 'I will take it, O Prophet Muhammad ﷺ,

101 *Sahih Bukhari* 3039.
102 *Al-Rawd al-Unuf* 3/267.
103 Ibid.
104 Ibid.
105 Ibid p.268.

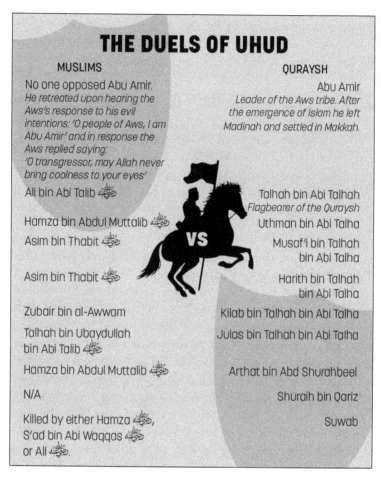

THE DUELS OF UHUD

MUSLIMS	QURAYSH
No one opposed Abu Amir. *He retreated upon hearing the Aws's response to his evil intentions: 'O people of Aws, I am Abu Amir' and in response the Aws replied saying: 'O transgressor, may Allah never bring coolness to your eyes'*	Abu Amir *Leader of the Aws tribe. After the emergence of Islam he left Madinah and settled in Makkah.*
Ali bin Abi Talib ﷺ	Talhah bin Abi Talhah *Flagbearer of the Quraysh*
Hamza bin Abdul Muttalib ﷺ	Uthman bin Abi Talha
Asim bin Thabit ﷺ	Musaf'i bin Talhah bin Abi Talha
Asim bin Thabit ﷺ	Harith bin Talhah bin Abi Talha
Zubair bin al-Awwam	Kilab bin Talhah bin Abi Talha
Talhah bin Ubaydullah bin Abi Talib ﷺ	Julas bin Talhah bin Abi Talha
Hamza bin Abdul Muttalib ﷺ	Arthat bin Abd Shurahbeel
N/A	Shuraih bin Qariz
Killed by either Hamza ﷺ, S'ad bin Abi Waqqas ﷺ or Ali ﷺ.	Suwab

and I will give it its right.' This courageous soul was none other than Abu Dujānah ﷺ.

The battle was launched and the customary duels began. As the two sides exchanged blows, Hind bin Utbah stood behind the men of the Quraysh, encouraging them and providing moral support by beating the drum.[106] As the battle took a leap, Abu Dujānah ﷺ fought his way through with the sword of Prophet Muhammad ﷺ. Likewise, Hamza ﷺ fought many Qurayshi leaders; none stood a chance against him. However, amidst the striking of

106 Ibid p.269.

swords, Wahshi, the slave of Jubayr bin Mut'im, waited for Hamza ﷺ, ready to attack him.[107] He had been given the offer of freedom if he carried out the deed of killing Hamza ﷺ. Hind eagerly waited for the fall of Hamza ﷺ, so that she could take vengeance for him killing her father and brother in the Battle of Badr. Hamza ﷺ was martyred by the striking spear of Wahshi. To satiate her desire for revenge, Hind later chewed on the liver and intestines of Hamza ﷺ and mutilated his body. The death of Hamza ﷺ was a great loss and source of grief to the Muslims that day.

On this day, many souls were taken, but the help of Allah was bestowed upon the Muslims as promised. The Quraysh were defeated, and the women escaped from the battle. However, upon seeing the Muslims triumph, the fifty archers who were still on post left their positions, hastening to collect the booty, despite being reprimanded by their commander. Instantly, the Quraysh attacked from the rear.

Amidst the chaos, a rumour spread that Prophet Muhammad ﷺ had died; this news gave advantage to the Quraysh to attack easily.[108] Little did they know that this report was false. During the battle, Prophet Muhammad ﷺ was injured by a rock, causing him to fall and lose his lower right lateral incisor and splitting his lower lip. Additionally, two metal links from the helmet of Muhammad ﷺ were thrust into his cheeks, causing great discomfort. Abu Ubayda bin Jarrah ﷺ lost his two teeth on removing the metal links from Prophet Muhammad's ﷺ blessed cheeks (may Allah be pleased with him).

When the Muslims realised that Prophet Muhammad ﷺ was still alive, they rushed towards him with surprise and joy. Umayyah bin Khalaf, a staunch enemy of Islam, caught up with Prophet Muhammad ﷺ and charged toward him. Prophet Muhammad ﷺ took the sword from one of his companions and struck Ubay, leaving him severely wounded.

Many others showed their love and sacrifice for Prophet Muhammad ﷺ. One of them was Abu Dujānah ﷺ, a courageous

107 Ibid p.271.
108 *Al-Rahīq ul-Makhtūm* p.228.

warrior who positioned himself before Prophet Muhammad ﷺ as his back faced the brutal enemy firing continuous arrows at him. Sa'd bin Ubadah ؓ shot arrows in defence of Prophet Muhammad ﷺ. As Prophet Muhammad ﷺ handed him the arrows, he exclaimed, 'May my father and mother be your ransom.'[109] One of the heroic warriors of that day was Hanzala bin Abu Amir al-Ghasīl ؓ, a newly married companion who left his house upon the call of jihad. He fought valiantly, pacing through the battlefield without any hesitation. He fought individuals such as Shadād bin al-Aswad and was close to killing Abu Sufyan.[110] Prophet Muhammad ﷺ said to his companions, 'Indeed, your companion has been bathed by the Angels.' The Companions asked what was its reason and he ﷺ replied, 'He left when he was in a state of *janabah*[111] upon hearing the call of *jihad*.'[112]

Like him, many others showed their wondrous love for Allah and His Messenger ﷺ, may Allah be pleased with them all. The battlefield became quiet, for it was now a graveyard of the martyred. Many great warriors lost their lives, the likes of Hamza ؓ, Ziyād bin As-Sakan ؓ, Anas bin Nadr ؓ and many other valiant warriors. Aisha ؓ and Umm Sulaym ؓ carried water to the survivors to quench their thirst as the Muslims located their martyred brothers. Before Abu Sufyan left, he announced from the heights of the mountain: 'Another battle the following year.'[113] After the burial, the Muslims returned to Madinah exhausted and wounded.

---

109 *Al-Rawd al-Unuf* 3/287.
110 Ibid p.278.
111 A state of major ritual impurity which requires a bath.
112 Ibid.
113 Ibid p.310.

GHAZWAH HAMRA AL-ASAD

Not satisfied after the battle of Uhud, Abu Sufyan wanted to
fight the Prophet Muhammad ﷺ once more.

Type:	Expedition
Date:	8th of Shawwal 3AH
Opposition:	Quraysh
No. of Muslims:	Same people that participated in the battle of Uhud
Muslims martyred:	2
No. of Unbelievers:	Survivors from Uhud
Unbelievers killed:	3
Prominent figures:	Abu Sufyan
Outcome:	No combat

Hamra al-Asad is situated eight to ten miles from Madinah on the left road, for anyone heading towards Zul-Hulayfah.[114] On the evening of the fifteenth of Shawwal, as the Quraysh returned from Uhud, they took refuge in an area called Rawha which is 36 miles from Madinah.[115] Reflecting on the battle, they believed that their mission was still incomplete and pending. They contemplated and concluded that since they had killed the majority of the companions of Prophet Muhammad ﷺ, why not launch a

114 *Zarqāni* 2/464.
115 *Al-Rahīq ul-Makhtūm* p.244.

Buwat

MADINAH

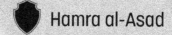 Hamra al-Asad

Safwan

ARABIA

Badr

final attack on Madinah? They assumed the Muslims would be exhausted and wounded from the recent battle, hence, they would be unable to survive another ambush.

However, this was not the attitude of all, as Safwan bin Uma-yyah deemed it wise to return to Makkah. He further exclaimed that Prophet Muhammad's ﷺ army was infused with zeal and devotion, therefore, there was a strong likelihood of them being unsuccessful in the attack. As this discussion was taking place, Prophet Muhammad ﷺ was made aware of the Qurayshi plan to attack. Instantly, he ﷺ despatched Bilal ؓ to alert the people of Madinah of the plan, and prepare them for battle. Prophet Muhammad ﷺ gave clear instructions for only the participants of Uhud to prepare and take part in this forthcoming war. The objective of this immediate action was to demonstrate to the Quraysh that the spirit and the energy[116] of the Muslims were still intact despite their injuries and exhaustion.

On Sunday the 16th of Shawwal, Prophet Muhammad ﷺ arrived at a location called Hamra al-Asad. Upon his entry, a leader of the Banu Khuza'ah tribe named Ma'bad Khuzai' paid a visit to Prophet Muhammad ﷺ. He offered Prophet Muhammad ﷺ his condolences and support on the defeat of the Muslims on the Battle of Uhud.[117] When Ma'bad left the presence of Prophet Muhammad ﷺ, he encountered Abu Sufyan and his army who expressed their intentions to attack Madinah. Ma'bad made Abu Sufyan aware of Prophet Muhammad's ﷺ presence in Hamra al-Asad and his powerful force ready to attack.[118] Upon hearing this, Abu Sufyan fled the area and returned to Makkah. Prophet Muhammad ﷺ, unaware of Abu Sufyan's escape, remained in Hamra al-Asad for three days[119] and left for Madinah on Friday. The following verse was revealed regarding this incident:

---

116 *Zarqāni* 2/466.
117 Ibid.
118 *Zarqāni* 2/467.
119 Ibid.

الَّذِينَ اسْتَجَابُوا لِلَّهِ وَالرَّسُولِ مِنْ بَعْدِ مَا أَصَابَهُمُ الْقَرْحُ لِلَّذِينَ أَحْسَنُوا مِنْهُمْ وَاتَّقَوْا أَجْرٌ عَظِيمٌ

And those who answered the call of Allah and His messenger after which harm had afflicted them, and for those who did good among them and feared Allah, there is a great reward [for them].[120]

120 Surah Al-Imran: 172.

GHAZWAH BANU NADIR

Amir bin Tufail had killed seventy Muslims, even though they had a peace treaty with Prophet Muhammad ﷺ. During this incident, the laws relating to the cutting down, burning of land and trees and the accumulation of booty during military conquest were sent down.

Type:	Expedition
Date:	Rabi' al-Awwal 4AH
Opposition:	Banu Nadir
No. of Muslims:	Unknown
Prominent figures:	Abu Bakr ؓ, Umar ؓ,
	Uthman bin Affan ؓ,
	Zubair ؓ, Talha ؓ,
	Abdur Rahman bin Awf ؓ,
	Sa'd bin Mu'az ؓ, Usaid bin Hudair
	ؓ; Sa'd bin Ubadah ؓ and others.
No. of Unbelievers:	Unknown
Outcome:	Muslims gained victory

Banu Nadir, a Jewish tribe that resided in the oasis of Madinah, were later banished from the city due to breaching the peace agreement with Prophet Muhammad ﷺ. Among the various opinions regarding the battle, Allama Suhayli highlights that it took place after the Battle of Badr. Similarly Allama Zuhri mentions this event to have occurred six months after Badr and before Uhud.[121]

121 *Zarqāni* 2/506.

ARABIA

· MADINAH
Banu Nadir

Red Sea

· Ghuran

· MAKKAH

After Bi'r Mauna, Amr bin Umayyah Damari ⬥, a survivor of the battle, was on a journey returning from the expedition when he crossed paths with two men from the Banu 'Āmir. After asking their identity, the three took refuge under the shade of a tree. Amr bin Umayyah fell into deep thought. He pondered over the death of seventy Muslims at the hands of Amir bin Tufail, the leader of the Banu 'Amir tribe. He considered how it would be impossible to avenge the death of all of them, but he would be able to avenge the death of some. With this thought, he killed two of the individuals that were in his presence. It should be noted that Amr bin Umayyah was oblivious to the fact that Prophet Muhammad ﷺ had made a peace treaty with the Banu 'Amir.[122]

When this news reached Prophet Muhammad ﷺ, he remarked that since they had made a peace treaty with this tribe, the blood money should be paid for the loss of the two individuals. Since the Banu Nadir were also an ally of the Banu 'Amir in terms of the peace treaty, it was also feasible to request the Banu Nadir to contribute to remitting the blood money to the Banu 'Amir. Prophet Muhammad ﷺ set out with a few companions, namely, Abu Bakr ⬥, Umar ⬥ and Ali ⬥,[123] to consult with the Banu Nadir concerning this matter.

Upon his arrival, Prophet Muhammad ﷺ was treated with courtesy and respect. The Banu Nadir instantly agreed upon contributing towards the blood money to Banu 'Āmir. In the meantime, the Banu Nadir had appointed a person to drop a boulder on Prophet Muhammad ﷺ to assassinate him. However, Sallam bin Miksham warned his fellow tribesmen of their stupidity in attempting to do so. He reminded them that Prophet Muhammad ﷺ would be notified by his Lord if they intended to carry out such a vile action. He also reiterated that they were bonded by a peace treaty with the Muslims and that such actions would breach the pact.[124] Moments later, Prophet Muhammad ﷺ was made aware of the treacherous actions of the Banu Nadir by Jibrīl ﷺ. Prophet Muhammad ﷺ left the gathering straight away and

---

122 *Al-Rawd al-Unuf* 3/412.
123 *Zarqāni* 2/509.
124 Ibid.

left his companions in their majlis, hastily returning to Madinah.[125] The Banu Nadir and the companions presumed Prophet Muhammad ﷺ to have left temporarily. However, a man named Kinanah bin Suwayrah highlighted the incident and exclaimed, 'Don't you know why Muhammad got up and left? By Allah, he was promptly informed about your treachery. By Allah, he is a messenger of Allah.'[126] As soon as the companions realised that Prophet Muhammad ﷺ was delayed in returning, they also got up in search of him towards Madinah. Ibn Aqabah says that the following verse was revealed regarding this incident:

$$\text{يَا أَيُّهَا الَّذِينَ آمَنُوا اذْكُرُوا نِعْمَتَ اللَّهِ عَلَيْكُمْ إِذْ هَمَّ قَوْمٌ أَنْ يَبْسُطُوا إِلَيْكُمْ}$$
$$\text{أَيْدِيَهُمْ فَكَفَّ أَيْدِيَهُمْ عَنْكُمْ وَاتَّقُوا اللَّهَ وَعَلَى اللَّهِ فَلْيَتَوَكَّلِ الْمُؤْمِنُونَ}$$

O you who believe, remember the blessings of your Lord upon you, when people were extending their hands upon you. He stopped their hands from you. Fear Allah and let the believers place their trust in Allah.[127]

Prophet Muhammad ﷺ shared the treacherous actions of the Banu Nadir as the reason for his sudden disappearance. He ﷺ appointed Abdullah bin Umm Makhtūm ؓ as the representative in Madinah and left to confront the Banu Nadir for their treacherous actions. The Banu Nadir were wary of Prophet Muhammad ﷺ, and so they locked themselves in their secure fortresses. To add to their arrogance, Abdullah bin Ubayy, the leader of the hypocrites, offered them his support. The Banu Nadir sent a message to Prophet Muhammad ﷺ with a seemingly sincere request. Their proposal consisted of the following: for Prophet Muhammad ﷺ to visit them with three of his companions so that they may converse with three of their rabbis. Their condition was that if after this discussion their rabbis accepted Islam, then they would follow suit. Amidst the chaos, the Banu Nadir privately advised their

125 *Al-Rawd al-Unuf* 3/413.
126 *Zarqāni* 3/509-510.
127 Surah Maidah: 11.

three rabbis to hide daggers in their clothing and to kill Prophet Muhammad ﷺ and his companions when they came into contact with them.[128]

Little did they know that this message had already reached Prophet Muhammad ﷺ. Their repeated malicious and deceptive actions left Prophet Muhammad ﷺ no choice but to attack them. According to Al-Waqīdi, the siege lasted for fifteen days.[129] Their palms and orchards were cut and burnt.[130] Eventually, as they endured a lot of loss, they begged for mercy. Prophet Muhammad ﷺ agreed to their request and commanded them to leave the city within ten days. He requested that they empty their homes and take their family members with them to settle elsewhere. They were also instructed to take as much wealth and contents as their camels could bear. There was a man amongst them who even ensured to take his door frame.[131] After a period of time, many of the Banu Nadir resided in Khaybar and some travelled to Syria.[132] The remaining goods were distributed amongst the Muhajirūn.[133] From amongst the tribe, two individuals came into the fold of Islam, one being Yamin bin Umair ؓ and the other Abu Saʿīd bin Wahhab ؓ.[134]

128 *Zarqāni* 2/510.
129 Ibid, p.511.
130 *Al-Rawd al-Unuf* 3/413.
131 Ibid, p.414.
132 Ibid.
133 Ibid.
134 Ibid p.415.

GHAZWAH DHATUR-RIQA'

Banu Maharib and Banu Tha'labah were amassing their troops in preparation for war against Prophet Muhammad ﷺ

Type:	Expedition
Date:	Jumada al-Ula 4AH,
	10th Muharram 5AH
Opposition:	Banu Maharib and Banu Tha'labah
No. of Muslims:	400 companions
No. of Unbelievers:	Allies of Banu Maharib and Banu
	Tha'labah
Outcome:	No combat

There are different opinions concerning the origin of the name Dhatur-Riqa'. The first opinion mentioned is that it refers to the name of a tree; others have explained *riqa'* to mean 'rags and patches', referring to the situation of Prophet Muhammad ﷺ and the companions whilst on this journey. It is further explained that due to the intense walking the soles of their feet became cracked, which they then had to wrap in cloth, hence its name. It has been narrated by Abu Musa al-Ash'ari ؓ who said: 'We set out for battle with the Messenger of Allah ﷺ. We were six soldiers and had only one camel between us which we rode on by turn. My feet were so badly injured that my nails dropped off. So we covered our feet with cloths. Hence, this expedition

• Khaybar

Dhatur-Riqa'

ARABIA

• MADINAH

• Badr

was called Dhatur-Riqa' (i.e., the expedition of rags).'[135] However, others are of the opinion that it has been named after a mountain where Prophet Muhammad ﷺ camped during this expedition. This mountain is known for its distinctive red, white, and black marks.[136]

As Jumada al-Ula commenced, Prophet Muhammad ﷺ was notified that the Banu Maharib and Tha'labah were collating troops to attack the Muslims and Prophet Muhammad ﷺ. With four hundred companions accompanying him, Prophet Muhammad ﷺ left Madinah towards a place called Najd. On his arrival, he encountered large troops of the Banu Ghatafan. Both parties drew closer; however, there was no physical combat. Indeed both parties feared each other until Prophet Muhammad ﷺ prayed Salahtul-Khawf (prayer for fear) with them. This changed their emotional state and rejuvenated their spirit:[137]

عَنْ يَزِيدَ بْنِ رُومَانَ، عَنْ صَالِحٍ، بْنِ خَوَّاتٍ عَمَّنْ صَلَّى مَعَ رَسُولِ اللهِ صلى الله عليه وسلم يَوْمَ ذَاتِ الرِّقَاعِ صَلَاةَ الْخَوْفِ أَنَّ طَائِفَةً صَفَّتْ مَعه وَطَائِفَةٌ وِجَاهَ الْعَدُوّ . فَصَلَّى بِالَّذِينَ مَعَهُ رَكْعَةً ثُمَّ ثَبَتَ قَائِمًا وَأَتَمُّوا لأَنْفُسِهِمْ . ثُمَّ انْصَرَفُوا فَصَفُّوا وِجَاهَ الْعَدُوّ وَجَاءَتِ الطَّائِفَةُ الأُخْرَى فَصَلَّى بِهِمُ الرَّكْعَةَ الَّتِي بَقِيَتْ ثُمَّ ثَبَتَ جَالِسًا وَأَتَمُّوا لأَنْفُسِهِمْ ثُمَّ سَلَّمَ بِهِمْ

It is narrated by Salih bin Khawwat from the one who prayed Salahtul-Khawf with Prophet Muhammad ﷺ on the day of Dhatur-Riqa', 'For indeed, a group formed a row and prayed along with him ﷺ, and a group faced the enemy. He led the group with him in a *rak'ah*, then remained standing whilst they completed their prayer by themselves. Then they left and formed a row facing the enemy. Then the second group came and he ﷺ led them in the other *rak'ah*, then he remained seated whilst

135 *Sahih Muslim* 1816, *Sahih Bukhari* 4128.
136 *Al-Rawd al-Unuf* 3/426.
137 Ibid p.427.

they finished their prayer and then he ﷺ did *taslīm*[138] with them.'[139]

During the course of this journey, Prophet Muhammad ﷺ and the companions sought shelter under trees to rest. A man from the Banu Muharib named Ghawrath said to his people from Ghatafan and Muharib: 'Shall I kill Muhammad for you?' They replied: 'Of course, but how will you kill him?' Ghawrath replied: 'By attacking him suddenly.' Ghawrath proceeded towards Prophet Muhammad ﷺ who was sitting with his sword in its sheath. Ghawrath said: 'Look, O Muhammad! Is this your sword?' He ﷺ said: 'Yes!' Ghawrath took the sword and withdrew it from its sheath; he swung it as if he intended to do something, and questioned mockingly whether he would be stopped by Allah. He said: 'O Muhammad, do you not fear me?' Prophet Muhammad ﷺ said: 'No, I do not fear of you.' Ghawrath replied: 'Do you not fear me, when I have in my hand this sword?' He ﷺ replied: 'No, Allah protects me from you.' Then the sword of Prophet Muhammad ﷺ fell from his hands and thereafter he ﷺ questioned Ghawrath similar to the way in which he had questioned him. Upon this, Allah the Most High revealed the verse:

يَا أَيُّهَا الَّذِينَ آمَنُوا اذْكُرُوا نِعْمَتَ اللَّهِ عَلَيْكُمْ إِذْ هَمَّ قَوْمٌ أَنْ يَبْسُطُوا إِلَيْكُمْ أَيْدِيَهُمْ فَكَفَّ أَيْدِيَهُمْ عَنْكُمْ ۖ وَاتَّقُوا اللَّهَ ۚ وَعَلَى اللَّهِ فَلْيَتَوَكَّلِ الْمُؤْمِنُونَ

O you who believe, remember the blessings of your Lord upon you, when people desired to harm but He stopped their hands from you. Fear Allah and let the believers place their trust in Allah.[140]

A similar incident transpired during the expedition of Ghatafan. Some have said the revelation possibly indicates the same

138 The concluding action of the Muslim prayer by saying السلام عليكم ورحمة الله to the right and then the left.
139 *Sahih Muslim* 839-843.
140 Surah Ma'idah: 11.

72

incident occurring at two different times; either the incident mentioned regarding the Prophet Muhammad ﷺ resting under a tree or the vent from Banu Nadir when a Jew intended to kill Prophet Muhammad ﷺ by throwing a rock at him. However, others say it is in reference to the same occasion.[141]

Soon after Prophet Muhammad ﷺ dismounted, he asked his companions, 'Who will cook for us?' In response, a man from the Muhajirūn and Ansār quickly stepped forward and volunteered to take on the responsibility of feeding Prophet Muhammad ﷺ and his companions. Prophet Muhammad ﷺ then instructed everyone to disperse into small groups; within his ﷺ group was Ammar and Abbad, may Allah be pleased with them. As Prophet Muhammad ﷺ left his small group he appointed Ammar bin Yasir ؓ, an Ansāri companion, and Abbad bin Bishr ؓ, a Muhajir companion, for the night watch. Between themselves, they decided that Abbad would keep guard for the first part of the night whilst Ammar for the latter.

As previously agreed upon, Ammar rested while Abbad took on night duty and engaged in prayer. During this time, an enemy took advantage of the situation and approached. When the enemy noticed Abbad's figure, he shot an arrow that pierced Abbad's body. Despite being in prayer and deeply absorbed in its sweetness, Abbad calmly removed the arrow, discarded it, and continued his prayer without showing any signs of pain or disturbance. The same incident occurred again in his salah, but Abbad remained steadfast without flinching. After the event happened for the third time, Abbad performed *rukū* (bowing) and *sujūd* (prostration) and then alerted Ammar. So Ammar told him to sit down as he had identified the enemy. Ammar immediately sprang up, and both companions recognized the man. The enemy, sensing the commotion, swiftly fled the scene.

When Ammar saw Abbad drenched in blood he said, 'All praise be to Allah!' He was perplexed by his situation and asked him, 'Why did you not caution me upon the first strike?' Abbad replied, 'I was reciting a surah from the Qur'an and I did not wish

141 *Zarqāni* 2/510.

to cut it short until I finished it. So when I was in *rukū* I heard you and I swear by Allah even if a lot of arrows were shot at me I would have continued, as Prophet Muhammad ﷺ commanded me that I control my *nafs* (inner-self) in salah from stopping until I finish my salah.'

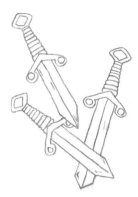

GHAZWAH AL-DAWMAT UL-JANDAL

Dawmat ul-Jandal was preparing to attack Madinah, but they scattered when they sensed the Muslim army.

Type:	Expedition
Date:	25th Rabi' al-Awwal, 5AH
Opposition:	Dawmat ul-Jandal
No. of Muslims:	1000 Companions
No. of Unbelievers:	Unknown
Outcome:	No combat

Dawmat ul-Jandal is a village in Jawf, located on the northern side of Saudi Arabia. Specifically, it is located to the left of Tayma, with a distance of approximately 450km.[142] Abu Ubaid al-Baqri has said that it was named after Dumah bin Isma'il.[143]

The event occurred during Rabi' al-Awwal, when Prophet Muhammad ﷺ received a message about some inhabitants of Dawmat ul-Jandal involved in a highway robbery and also planning to attack Madinah.[144] Prophet Muhammad ﷺ appointed Siba' bin Arfatah Al-Ghifari as the keeper of Madinah.[145] With an army of one thousand men, Prophet Muhammad ﷺ set out for Dawmat

142 *Al-Rawd al-Unuf* 3/441.
143 Ibid.
144 *Al-Rahīq ul-Makhtūm* p.257, *Zarqāni* 2/540.
145 *Al-Rawd al-Unuf* 3/441.

SYRIA

Dawmat ul-Jandal

Tabuk

ARABIA

Khaybar

Red Sea

MADINAH

ul-Jandal with only five days of Rabi' al-Awwal remaining.[146] In order to hasten the journey, Prophet Muhammad ﷺ sought assistance from a man named Madqur al-Udhari[147] from the Banu Udhrah to be their guide for the road. Upon their arrival, Prophet Muhammad ﷺ realised that the inhabitants of Dawmat ul-Jandal had already fled the area and dispersed into different localities before his arrival.[148] He ﷺ thereafter sent groups to search for the inhabitants; however, none could be located except for their shepherds and cattle which were captured. En route to Madinah, Prophet Muhammad ﷺ made a peace treaty with Uyaynah bin Hisn.[149] Despite there being no physical combat, Prophet Muhammad ﷺ managed to secure the localities and make peace within the area, resulting in the Quraysh and Jews becoming more vigilant of their actions. Finally, after a tiresome journey, Prophet Muhammad ﷺ entered Madinah on the twentieth of Rabi' ath-Thani.

---

146 *Zarqāni* 2/540.
147 Ibid.
148 Ibid.
149 *Al-Rahīq ul-Makhtūm* p.257.

GHAZWAH AL-MURAYSI'

Harith bin Abi Dirar, the leader of Banu Mustaliq, prepared a combat against the Prophet Muhammad ﷺ.

Type:	Expedition
Other names:	Banu Mustaliq
Date:	Monday 2nd Sha'ban 6AH
Opposition:	Banu Mustaliq
No. of Muslims:	Companions with 30 horses
No. of Unbelievers:	Unknown
Unbelievers killed:	10 men were killed, 2000 camels and 5000 goats were seized, and 200 families were captured by the Muslims
Prominent figures:	Harith bin Abi Dirar
Outcome:	Muslims gained victory

The Banu Mustaliq are from the Jews of Madinah; they were the Banu Jazīmah bin Ka'b bin Khuza'ah, a forceful party with a very loud voice.[150] The title Muraysi' is derived from the name of a water spring or pond belonging to the Khuza'ah near an area named Qadīd which is approximately 120km along the route from Makkah to Madinah. Muraysi' is said to be further from the seashore inwardly but about 80km closer to Sif al-Bahr.[151]

150 *Al-Rawd al-Unuf* 4/16.
151 Ibid.

Note: As this location no longer exists on the original site, this is an educated guess based on information provided by scholars.

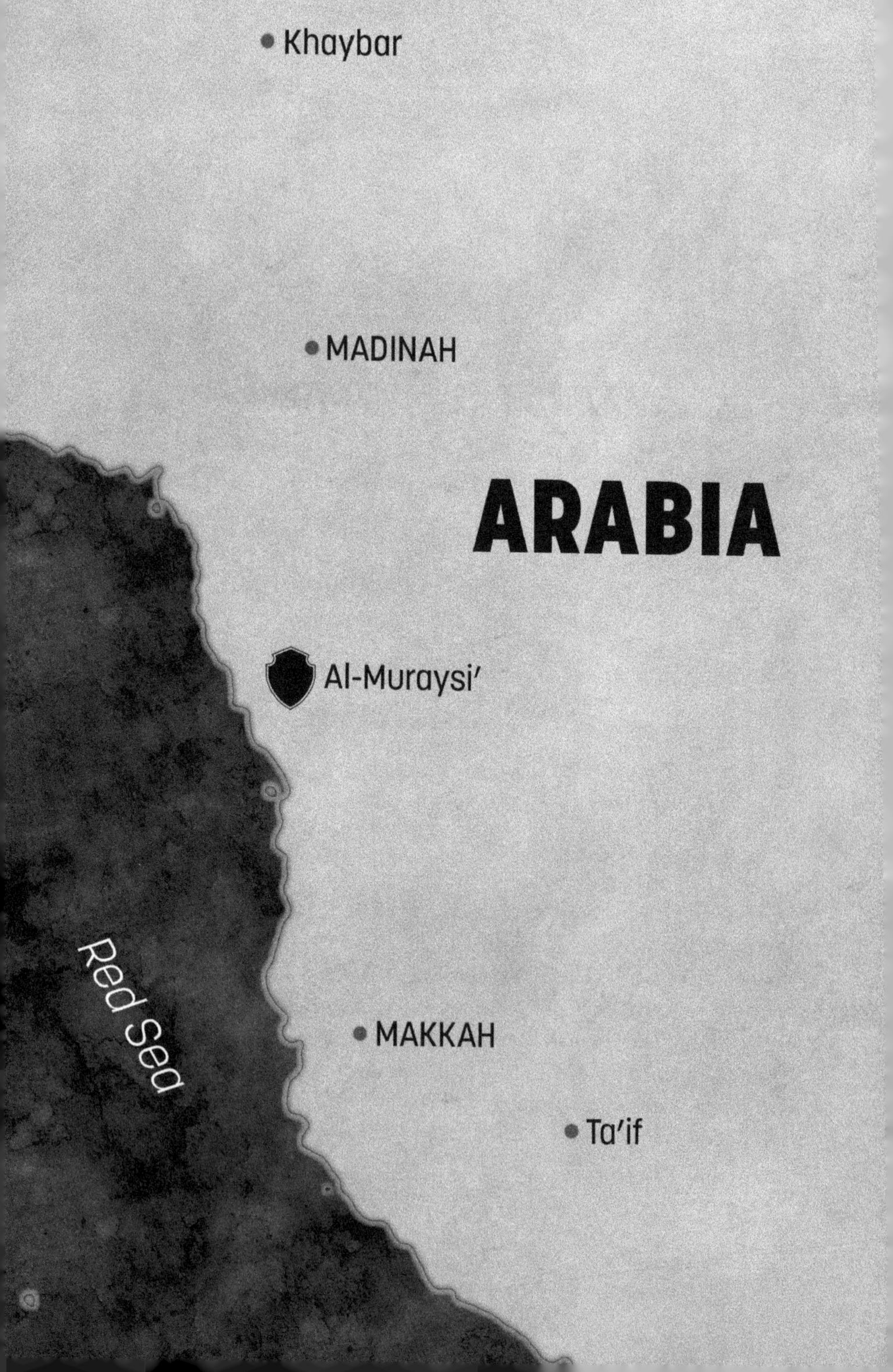

Khaybar

MADINAH

ARABIA

Al-Muraysi'

Red Sea

MAKKAH

Ta'if

Prophet Muhammad ﷺ was notified that Harith bin Abi Dirar, leader of the Banu Mustaliq and father of Juwayriyah bint Harith ؓ who later became the wife of Prophet Muhammad ﷺ, was amassing a troop to attack the Muslims. Prophet Muhammad ﷺ sent a messenger named Buraydah bin Hasīb Al-Aslami ؓ to investigate the truth of the matter. As soon as the affirmation was sent, Prophet Muhammad ﷺ began to prepare for battle.[152]

The companions ؓ were prepared and upon the command of Prophet Muhammad ﷺ an army set out with thirty horses, twenty belonging to the Ansār and ten to the Muhajirūn.[153] Ibn Sa'd mentions that there were twenty Muhajirūn and twenty Ansār.[154] With the aspiration to gain a high amount of booty, the hypocrites joined the Muslims in the expedition. Their contribution was only in hope that the Muslims would be victorious again as in previous battles. The majority of the soldiers were of the Munafiqūn (hypocrites); there is no other battle the likes of this where the hypocrites also joined the Muslim army.[155]

On Monday the second of Sha'ban 6AH,[156] Prophet Muhammad ﷺ set out for battle, leaving Abu Dhar al-Ghifari ؓ as his representative in Madinah. Another opinion suggests that Numaylah bin Abdullah al-Laythi ؓ was appointed as the representative.[157] Prophet Muhammad ﷺ was accompanied by two of his wives on this expedition, Aisha ؓ and Umm Salamah ؓ. The Muslim army paced to the battlefield, leaving the Banu Mustaliq baffled as they were engaged in watering their animals. The following has been mentioned in Sahih al-Bukhari:

حَدَّثَنَا عَلِيُّ بْنُ الْحَسَنِ، أَخْبَرَنَا عَبْدُ اللَّهِ، أَخْبَرَنَا ابْنُ عَوْنٍ، قَالَ كَتَبْتُ إِلَى نَافِعٍ فَكَتَبَ إِلَىَّ أَنَّ النَّبِيَّ صلى الله عليه وسلم أَغَارَ عَلَى بَنِي الْمُصْطَلِقِ

152 *Al-Rahīq ul-Makhtūm* p.280, *Zarqāni* 3/5.
153 *Umdatul Qari* 17/269.
154 *Zarqāni* 3/5.
155 Ibid p.5.
156 Ibid p.4.
157 *Al-Rawd al-Unuf* 4/16.

وَهُمْ غَارُونَ وَأَنْعَامُهُمْ تُسْقَى عَلَى الْمَاءِ، فَقَتَلَ مُقَاتِلَتَهُمْ، وَسَبَى ذَرَارِيَّهُمْ،

وَأَصَابَ يَوْمَئِذٍ جُوَيْرِيَةَ. حَدَّثَنِي بِهِ عَبْدُ اللَّهِ بْنُ عُمَرَ، وَكَانَ فِي ذَلِكَ

الْجَيْشِ

Ibn Awn narrated that: 'I wrote to Nafi' and he [Nafi'] wrote in reply to me that Prophet Muhammad ﷺ attacked the Banu Mustaliq whilst they were unaware and [occupied] in watering their cattle at the place of water. Their warriors were killed, their children and women were taken as captives; this is the day Muhammad ﷺ got Juwayriyah.'[158]

As soon as the army reached the designated area, Prophet Muhammad ﷺ split the army into two groups. Abu Bakr ؓ carried the flag for the Muhajirūn, whereas Sa'd ibn Ubadah carried the flag for the Ansār.[159] As the two armies gathered around the well of Muraysi', both engaged in constant arrow shooting.[160] Being unable to defend against the sudden assault, ten men were killed and the remaining children and elderly were taken as prisoners.[161] Ibn Sa'd mentions that it was a total of two hundred families. The wealth left over was taken as booty alongside a total of two thousand camels and five thousand goats.[162] Amongst the captives was Juwayriyah ؓ, daughter of Harith ibn Abi Dirar, the chief of the Banu Mustaliq. Upon Prophet Muhammad's ﷺ marriage to her, a hundred of the prisoners accepted Islam. Aisha ؓ narrates the incident of when Prophet Muhammad ﷺ freed and married Juwayriyah ؓ as follows:

عَنْ عَائِشَةَ، - رَضِيَ الله عنها - قَالَتْ وَقَعَتْ جُوَيْرِيَةُ بِنْتُ الْحَارِثِ بْنِ

الْمُصْطَلِقِ فِي سَهْمِ ثَابِتِ بْنِ قَيْسِ بْنِ شَمَّاسٍ أَوِ ابْنِ عَمٍّ لَهُ فَكَاتَبَتْ

عَلَى نَفْسِهَا وَكَانَتِ امْرَأَةً مَلَّاحَةً تَأْخُذُهَا الْعَيْنُ - قَالَتْ عَائِشَةُ رضي الله

158 *Sahih Bukhari* 2541.
159 *Zarqāni* 3/6.
160 *Fath ul-Bari* 7/538.
161 *Al-Rawd al-Unuf* 4/16.
162 *Zarqāni* 3/7.

عنها - فَجَاءَتْ تَسْأَلُ رَسُولَ اللَّهِ صلى الله عليه وسلم فِي كِتَابَتِهَا فَلَمَّا قَامَتْ
عَلَى الْبَابِ فَرَأَيْتُهَا كَرِهْتُ مَكَانَهَا وَعَرَفْتُ أَنَّ رَسُولَ اللَّهِ صلى الله عليه
وسلم سَيَرَى مِنْهَا مِثْلَ الَّذِي رَأَيْتُ فَقَالَتْ يَا رَسُولَ اللَّهِ أَنَا جُوَيْرِيَةُ بِنْتُ
الْحَارِثِ وَإِنَّمَا كَانَ مِنْ أَمْرِي مَا لاَ يَخْفَى عَلَيْكَ وَإِنِّي وَقَعْتُ فِي سَهْمِ
ثَابِتِ بْنِ قَيْسِ بْنِ شَمَّاسٍ وَإِنِّي كَاتَبْتُ عَلَى نَفْسِي فَجِئْتُكَ أَسْأَلُكَ فِي
كِتَابَتِي فَقَالَ رَسُولُ اللَّهِ صلى الله عليه وسلم " فَهَلْ لَكِ إِلَى مَا هُوَ خَيْرٌ
مِنْهُ " . قَالَتْ وَمَا هُوَ يَا رَسُولَ اللَّهِ قَالَ " أُوَدِّي عَنْكِ كِتَابَتَكِ وَأَتَزَوَّجُكِ
" . قَالَتْ قَدْ فَعَلْتُ قَالَتْ فَتَسَامَعَ - تَعْنِي النَّاسَ - أَنَّ رَسُولَ اللَّهِ صلى الله
عليه وسلم قَدْ تَزَوَّجَ جُوَيْرِيَةَ فَأَرْسَلُوا مَا فِي أَيْدِيهِمْ مِنَ السَّبْيِ فَأَعْتَقُوهُمْ
وَقَالُوا أَصْهَارُ رَسُولِ اللَّهِ صلى الله عليه وسلم فَمَا رَأَيْنَا امْرَأَةً كَانَتْ أَعْظَمَ
بَرَكَةً عَلَى قَوْمِهَا مِنْهَا أُعْتِقَ فِي سَبِيهَا مِائَةُ أَهْلِ بَيْتٍ مِنْ بَنِي الْمُصْطَلِقِ

Aisha ﷺ narrates that Juwayriyah, daughter of al-Harith ibn al-Mustaliq, fell into the share of Thabit ibn Qays ibn Shammas, or to her cousin. She agreed to a contract to purchase her freedom. She was a very handsome woman and very pleasing to the eye. Aisha ﷺ said: 'She came to ask Prophet Muhammad ﷺ regarding the purchase of her freedom. As she was standing by the door, I looked at her with dislike. I understood that Prophet Muhammad ﷺ would look at her in the same manner as I looked at her. She said: "O Muhammad ﷺ, I am Juwayriyah, daughter of al-Harith, and a matter has befallen that which is not concealed from you. I have fallen into the share of Thabit ibn Qays ibn Shammas, and I have entered into an agreement to purchase my freedom. I have come to you to ask about the purchase of my freedom." Prophet Muhammad ﷺ said: "I have something which is better than it." She asked: "What is that, O Prophet Muhammad ﷺ?" He ﷺ replied: "I will pay the price of your freedom on your behalf, and I will marry you." She said:

"Indeed I will do this." She (Aisha) said: The people then heard that Prophet Muhammad ﷺ had married Juwayriyah. They released the captives under their possession and set them free, and said: They are the relatives of Prophet Muhammad ﷺ through marriage. We did not see any woman greater than Juwayriyah who brought blessings to her people. One hundred families of Banu al-Mustaliq were set free due to her[163] [marriage with Prophet Muhammad ﷺ].'

Since this was the first expedition the hypocrites participated in, they found every opportunity to create havoc. It has been recorded in Ibn Hisham that when Prophet Muhammad ﷺ and the companions camped near the well, a worker of Umar ibn al-Khattab ؓ named Jahjah bin Mas'ud from the Banu Ghifar tribe steered his horse towards the opening of the water, blocking its access from Sinan bin Wabir al-Juhani, an ally of the Banu Awf bin Khazraj. This angered him and a quarrel broke out. Juhani shouted, 'O people of the Ansār!' And Jahjah shouted, 'O people of the Muhajirūn!' This angered Abdullah ibn Ubayy bin Sulūl and he addressed the group before him. 'Oh, look what they have done! They have shunned us and outnumbered us in our land!' he bellowed with disgust. 'By Allah, we will not return until we have crushed them and just like the saying "If you fatten your dog it will eat you!" Swear by Allah when we return to Madinah the most honourable will expel the unworthy out from Madinah.'[164] When Muhammad ﷺ heard of this, he reprimanded it and remarked: 'These are the practices of *jahiliyah* (days of ignorance).' Zaid bin Arqam, a servant who witnessed the incident, informed Prophet Muhammad ﷺ of this event upon which Umar ؓ remarked, 'Bring Abbad ibn Bishr and tell him to kill him (Abdullah ibn Ubayy).' In response, Prophet Muhammad ﷺ told Umar ؓ that it would be wiser to dismiss the matter as it would be proclaimed that 'Muhammad kills his companions.'

A similar narration has been mentioned in Jami' at-Tirmidhi with the addition of the quarrel breaking out due to a Muhājir

163 *Sunan Abi Dawud* 3931.
164 *Al-Rawd al-Unuf* 4/17.

kicking an Ansār.[165] Soon after this event, Prophet Muhammad ﷺ decided within an hour of camping to announce to the troops to start moving ahead.[166] Prophet Muhammad ﷺ began to walk with his people from that very day till evening and from night till morning. This became their routine until sunrise; there was not a single person who was not overcome by sleepiness and exhaustion. Indeed, the wisdom behind Prophet Muhammad's ﷺ actions was to occupy the mind of the Muslims and to divert their attention from the incident which occurred the previous day relating to Abdullah ibn Ubayy.

The incident of *ifk* can be regarded as one of the most challenging events for Prophet Muhammad ﷺ. The term *ifk* according to the Arabic lexicon refers to a false statement which damages someone's reputation. This incident has been mentioned in detail within the Sahihayn.[167] The following is a summary of the event.

The incident of the slander against Aisha ؓ transpired whilst returning from this expedition. During the lengthy journey Aisha ؓ went to answer the call of nature in a secluded area. Upon her return, her Yemeni onyx necklace fell apart. She preoccupied herself with searching for the pieces and got delayed. After she found the beads, she returned to an empty camp; her companions had left her behind. She remained at the same location in hope that they would come and find her. As she waited, she covered herself and fell asleep. Safwan bin Mu'attal al-Sulami ؓ was given the job of retrieving any valuables left behind by the army. As he passed by the camp, he noticed Aisha ؓ. He was able to recognise her as he had seen her before the ruling of covering was enforced. Safwan bin Mu'attal al-Sulami ؓ recited *Inna lillahi wa inna ilayhi raji'ūn* (Indeed, to Allah we belong and to Him we return). Upon his remark Aisha ؓ jolted awake and instantly covered her face. He spoke to her of nothing more but directed her towards a kneeling camel, after which he moved away. She steered the reins of the camel and headed towards the camp. Abdullah bin Ubayy saw Aisha ؓ and Mu'attal al-Sulami entering the locality of the

165 *Jami' at-Tirmidhi* 3631.
166 *Al-Rawd al-Unuf* 4/17-18.
167 *Sahih Bukhari* 4141, *Sahih Muslim* and *Sahih Bukhari*.

85

campers later on during the day. This aroused a thought in his mind to spread a rumour and to question the chastity of Aisha ﷺ. This rumour caused havoc and dismay in the community, even affecting the relationship between Aisha ﷺ and her family members. As it is said, truth prevails, and in this case her innocence and modesty were retained and justice was given to her by Allah Himself in the Qur'an. May Allah be pleased with her.

GHAZWAH AL-KHANDAQ

Abu Sufyan threatened the Muslims that he would return the following year after Uhud to attack them. Due to the bad storm during the battle, the Quraysh were scared and confused and so they fled from the battlefield. The participation of Prophet Muhammad ﷺ in digging the trench teaches us the humbleness a leader should have, as well as the attention he should pay when executing a plan. The benefits of Mashwarah and team involvement is evident within this battle.

Type:	Battle
Other names:	Ahzab
Date:	28th or 27th Shawwal 5AH
Opposition:	Abu Sufyan and his force
No. of Muslims:	3,000 companions
Muslims martyred:	Light loss, including Sa'd bin Mu'az ﷺ, Anas bin Uwais ﷺ, Abdullah bin Sahl ﷺ, Tufail bin Nu'man ﷺ, Tha'labah bin Anamah ﷺ, Ka'b bin Zaid ﷺ. The last two names have been added by Hafiz Dimyati: Qais bin Zaid ﷺ, Abdullah bin Abi Khalid ﷺ
No. of Unbelievers:	10,000 men
Unbelievers killed:	Heavy loss, including Nawfal bin Abdullah, Amr bin Abduwudd, Maniyah bin Ubaid
Outcome:	No combat

ARABIA

Khandaq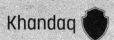

• MADINAH

Safwan •

• Badr

Khandaq literally means a ditch/trench, and it is due to its distinct war strategy of digging a trench that this battle is referred to as such. Another name designated to this battle is Ahzab, which translates as confederates, parties or union. This alludes to the union of particular tribes from the disbelievers with the intention to rebel against Prophet Muhammad ﷺ and to also sever pacts previously made with him.[168]

There is a lengthy discussion amongst scholars regarding the year of its occurrence. Some esteemed scholars such as Musa bin Uqbah and Malik are of the opinion that it transpired in Shawwal 4AH. However, Ahmad and Ibn Ishaq suggest 5AH to be the correct year. Furthermore, Ibn Sa'd mentions it to be specifically on Monday Dhul-Qa'dah 5AH for the duration of eight nights after the battle of Uhud.[169] Similarly, there is a difference in opinion on how long the disbelievers resided in Khandaq. The number of nights or days varies from ten to twenty, with twenty days being the dominant opinion.[170]

On his return from Uhud, Abu Sufyan made threats to the Muslims that he would return to fight them the following year. When the following year commenced he set out with an army, but due to the difficult circumstances of drought he deemed it wise to return to Makkah. After the banishment of the Banu Nadir, Huyayy bin Akhtab went to Makkah to lure the Quraysh to fight against Prophet Muhammad ﷺ. Kinanah bin Rab'i also approached the Banu Ghatafan and persuaded them to take up arms against Prophet Muhammad ﷺ and the Muslims. Kinanah offered a deal to the Banu Ghatafan, promising to give them the produce of palms annually if they agreed to the condition. Upon hearing about the deal and what it entailed, Uyaynah bin Hisn promptly agreed. A year later, he amassed an army of ten thousand men to march towards Madinah for the battle of Khandaq.[171]

Cold weather crept through the mountain passes and bitter wind tore its way through the air. Back in Madinah, Prophet

168 *Fath ul-Bari* 7/491.
169 *Umdat ul-Qari* 237/17.
170 *Fath ul-Bari* 7/492.
171 Ibid p.491.

Muhammad ﷺ gathered the companions for consultation. Salman al-Farisi ؓ proposed the idea of digging trenches around the city. He affirmed that it would be exhausting and difficult to fight them on an open field. Fighting them with the protection of the trench would be advantageous. This impressive idea ignited a spark of hope and joy for the Muslims, as it appealed to everyone and Prophet Muhammad ﷺ.

This was the severest battle fought by the Muslims as they were facing a large army of twelve to fifteen thousand whereas the Muslims were only three thousand in number and poorly equipped.[172] Another factor that escalated the situation was the bitingly cold weather. Despite the difficulties faced whilst digging the trench, the call for consultation benefitted the Muslims in two ways: to establish the Sunnah, and also to unite the hearts of the Muslims and support each other at a time of need. No time was spared. Prophet Muhammad ﷺ set the boundaries and assigned a group of ten people per trench. They were appointed to dig ten feet deep into the ground. There is a difference of opinion regarding how long it took to dig these trenches. Scholars such as Ibn Ishaq and Musa have mentioned it took approximately twenty nights whilst al-Waqīdi claims it took twenty-four days. However, twenty days was the actual time span of the entire siege.[173]

The hypocrites' negligent attitude during the digging of the trench slowed the progress down. Ibn Hisham mentions that when the work would resume, the hypocrites would disappear and return to their families; however, when the Muslims would ask Prophet Muhammad ﷺ to even relieve themselves they would return to work as soon as they were free.[174]

The trench began from Shaikhayn as far as the western corner of Mount Sal' and was later extended to the intersections of the valley of Buthān and Ratāuna.[175] Prophet Muhammad ﷺ also participated in the digging. As he struck the ground for the first time, he proclaimed, 'We commence in the name of Allah. If we

172 Ibid.
173 *Fath ul-Bari* 7/492.
174 *Al-Rawd al-Unuf* 3/444.
175 *Ma'riful Qur'an*, Surah Ahzab pp.106-107.

are submissive to anyone other than Him, then we are doomed. Oh, how excellent is our Lord and how excellent is our religion!'[176] As the Ansār and Muhajirūn devoted themselves to digging the trench, to boost their confidence and infuse their spirits with energy, they would recite many verses such as, 'O Allah! There is no life other than the life of the hereafter. So pardon the Ansār and Muhajirūn.'[177]

As the companions busied themselves with digging the trenches they were confronted by a problem. A giant boulder was found and when this issue was raised to Prophet Muhammad ﷺ, unlike any other leader, he replied: 'Wait, I will go down into the trench myself.' It is important to acknowledge that Prophet Muhammad ﷺ and the companions had not eaten in three days. Prophet Muhammad ﷺ tied stones to his abdomen to contain the hunger. Jabir ؓ narrates: 'Prophet Muhammad ﷺ gripped the axe with his blessed hands and struck the boulder, turning it into a mound of sand.'[178] The details of this event have been mentioned in Sahih Bukhari.[179] On the first strike Prophet Muhammad ﷺ pronounced 'Allahu Akbar' and remarked that he had been awarded the keys of Syria. On the second strike he pronounced 'Allahu Akbar' and remarked that he had been awarded the keys of Persia and on the third blow, that he was awarded the keys of Yemen. All these materialised later on, as the lands were conquered and taken under the rule of Islam.[180]

The trenches were incomplete when ten thousand Qurayshi warriors landed on the outskirts of Madinah. They chose their land and camped near Uhud. With an army of three thousand companions, Prophet Muhammad ﷺ set out to confront them and chose Mount Sila' as their meeting point. The trenches put a barrier between both parties. Prophet Muhammad ﷺ sent the women and children to the fortresses for security. An idea struck the mind of Huyayy bin Akhtab, leader of the Banu Nadir. He

---

176 *Zarqāni* 3/29-30.
177 Ibid p.24.
178 *Fath ul-Bari* 7/304-5.
179 *Sahih Bukhari* 4101.
180 *Al-Rawd al-Unuf* 3/447-448.

wanted everyone to turn against Prophet Muhammad ﷺ and the Muslims. In order to do this, he needed the Banu Qurayzah on his side; however, they had already made a peace treaty with Prophet Muhammad ﷺ. Huyayy visited Ka'b bin Asad[181] and upon seeing his arrival he slammed the door shut. Huyayy shouted, 'Open the door.' Ka'b responded, 'Pity on you, O Huyayy! Indeed you are an unfortunate man. I have already accepted the pact of Prophet Muhammad ﷺ and I will not breach the law, because I have not witnessed anything from him other than truthfulness, loyalty, and fulfilment of his promises.' Huyayy was not a man to give up easily, so he further pleaded, 'Give me permission to present before you something which guarantees you eternal honour. I am accompanied by the forces of Quraysh and Ghatafan right to your doorstep, all of whom have promised not to surrender until they have eradicated Muhammad and his companions.' Ka'b replied 'By Allah! You always bring misfortune to your actions. I will not breach the pact I made with Prophet Muhammad ﷺ, because I have not witnessed anything from him other than truthfulness, loyalty, and fulfilment of his promises.' Huyayy continued to persuade using his tactics, until he convinced Ka'b to break the pact with Prophet Muhammad ﷺ.

When Prophet Muhammad ﷺ received this message he sent Sa'd bin Mu'az, Sa'd bin Ubadah and Abdullah bin Rawahah رضى الله عنهم to enquire about the situation. He also mentioned to them, 'If the news is affirmative then inform me in such a way that no being is able to fathom its meaning. And if it is incorrect, if you reveal it publicly then there is no problem as the news is false.' When the group returned with the message they merely said, 'Adal and Qarah,'[182] meaning that they have also betrayed us like the tribes of Adal and Qarah. Prophet Muhammad ﷺ understood their indication. Two weeks passed without any actual combat, other than both sides lobbing arrows at each other.

In the eleventh hour, a few mounted warriors from the Quraysh took off to fight the Muslims. From amongst them were

181 Ibid, pp.449-450.
182 *Zarqāni* 3/38-39.

Amr bin Abduwudd, 'Ikrimah bin Abi Jahl, Hubairah bin Abi Wahab, Dirār bin Khatab and Nawfal bin Abdullah. As soon as they reached the trenches they were baffled, and exclaimed, 'By Allah! We have never had such deceptive tactics amongst the Arabs before this.' Due to one corner of the trench being narrow, a few men from the Quraysh were able to cross the barrier. As they entered the border of the Muslims, they challenged them to engage in one-to-one combat. Amr bin Abduwudd came charging forward. Enveloped in armour from head to toe, he exclaimed: 'Is there anyone who dares to take me on?' Upon this remark, Ali ؓ replied, 'O Amr, I call you unto Allah and His Messenger. I invite you towards Islam.' Amr was not interested in accepting Islam; he had only one thought on his mind and that was to annihilate the Muslims. As soon as Ali ؓ accepted to fight him, he told Ali ؓ how he did not desire to kill youngsters. Ali ؓ was adamant and replied, 'But I would love to kill you.' This enraged Amr, so he dismounted his horse and marched towards Ali ؓ and their combat began. With a slight wound on his forehead from Amr's sword, Ali ؓ launched his final attack and killed him.

Amidst the victory and the Muslims triumphing over this adversary, Nawfal, another member of the Quraysh, galloped towards Prophet Muhammad ﷺ to kill him. As he leaped over the trench, he fell in and broke his neck. The day passed with both parties shooting arrows and striking blows against one another.

Amidst all the commotion, a chief from Banu Ghatafan named Nu'aym bin Mas'ud Al-Ashja'i presented himself before Prophet Muhammad ﷺ to embrace Islam. After his acceptance, he asked Prophet Muhammad ﷺ how he could serve Islam. In response, he ﷺ advised him to return to his people and if possible to take any action in defence of Islam whilst he was still able to. Nu'aym devised a very shrewd strategy which resulted in the Banu Qurayzah withdrawing the support they had offered to the Quraysh.[183] His plan unfolded as follows. Nu'aym ؓ first visited the Banu Qurayzah, with whom he had old connections since the Days of Ignorance. He told them that if they considered him

183 The details of this incident are mentioned in *Al-Rawd al-Unuf* 3/462-464.

a good friend of theirs then to heed his advice and not partake in the battle with Prophet Muhammad ﷺ since if the Quraysh, Banu Ghatafan, or other Jewish tribes were defeated they would not be in much loss as Madinah was not their home. However, if the Banu Qurayzah faced defeat they would be stripped of their home and a situation would arise in which some of their chiefs would be up for ransom and then escape, leaving them all at the mercy of the Muslims. He reassured them that it would be wise to pull back from this battle. The Banu Qurayzah were content with Nu'aym's suggestion and they also appreciated his advice. Soon after, Nu'aym ؓ went to the Quraysh and said, 'I am a friend of yours and also a well-wisher. I have come with some news which in return I ask for you not to disclose my identity.' He informed them that the Banu Qurayzah regretted their earlier decision and had sent a message to Prophet Muhammad ﷺ, offering to assist him. However, the Banu Qurayzah planned to betray the chiefs from the Banu Ghatafan and Quraysh by passing them on to be killed before joining the battle themselves. Additionally, the Banu Qurayzah demanded that these chiefs be given to them for ransom, leaving their intentions unclear. Nu'aym ؓ sent the same message to the Banu Ghatafan and as a result, their plan to fight Prophet Muhammad ﷺ was a complete disaster.

Abu Sufyan sent two representatives from the Quraysh and the Banu Qurayzah to the Banu Ghatafan, notifying them that their war supplies were deteriorating and their soldiers were becoming tired of fighting, thus, they were looking forward to their participation in the battle. In response, the Banu Ghatafan said that they would ask for some of their chiefs to be kept in their custody as a deal. When this message reached Abu Sufyan, he sent another message saying that they have a choice to take part in the battle or not; however, none of their men would be given to them as ransom. All the tribes gained confidence in the advice of Nu'aym ؓ and so their plan to work together against Prophet Muhammad ﷺ lapsed.

As they say, nothing can change your destiny except supplication to Allah. The beloved of Allah ﷺ devoted his time to making supplication and he sought Allah's aid to shower His divine assistance. Allah the Most High accepted his supplication and caused a fierce wind to blow across the tents of Banu Ghatafan and the Quraysh. There was chaos and havoc. As the Quraysh started retreating, Prophet Muhammad ﷺ remarked: 'Now we will attack them and they will not attack us.'[184] As soon as the sound of victory echoed through the land, the hypocrites fled to success and sought their share from the booty. Allah mentions this action of theirs in Surah Ahzāb:

$$ أَشِحَّةً عَلَيْكُمْ ۖ فَإِذَا جَاءَ ٱلْخَوْفُ رَأَيْتَهُمْ يَنظُرُونَ إِلَيْكَ تَدُورُ أَعْيُنُهُمْ كَٱلَّذِى يُغْشَىٰ عَلَيْهِ مِنَ ٱلْمَوْتِ ۖ فَإِذَا ذَهَبَ ٱلْخَوْفُ سَلَقُوكُم بِأَلْسِنَةٍ حِدَادٍ أَشِحَّةً عَلَى ٱلْخَيْرِ ۚ أُوْلَـٰئِكَ لَمْ يُؤْمِنُوا۟ فَأَحْبَطَ ٱللَّهُ أَعْمَـٰلَهُمْ ۚ وَكَانَ ذَٰلِكَ عَلَى ٱللَّهِ يَسِيرًا $$

> [And they are] unwilling against you. But when fear comes, you
> will see them looking towards you, rolling their eyes, like the
> ones who get faint due to death. Then once the fear has gone.
> They attack you with sharp tongues, in greed for the good. These
> people did not accept the faith (in real terms), therefore Allah
> has made worthless their deeds and that is easy for Allah.[185]

This exemplifies the cowardice of the hypocrites and their greed for wealth even though they did not take part in any labour. However, when the Muslims enjoyed the spoils of war they claimed their share as they reinforced that the Muslims would not have succeeded without their help.

'It is narrated by Hudhayfah ؓ that Prophet Muhammad ﷺ said, "Who will bring me news of the opposing party and in return will receive Paradise?" No one volunteered for this difficult job. As a result, Prophet Muhammad ﷺ appointed me to carry out the very important task; like others, I too was very scared. When I reached the camp of Abu Sufyan, he gathered the people to announce some important news; however, he first requested

---

184 *Sahih Bukhari* 4109.
185 Surah Ahzab: 19.

everyone to ensure they recognised the person sitting beside them as he worried about there being spies amongst them.' Hudhayfah ؓ mentions that at this point he became worried about being recognised and so he cleverly slapped the hand of the man sitting next to him before he could ask him about his identity. The opponent replied saying, 'It's funny how you do not know me,' and he identified himself. Like so, by the mercy of Allah, Hudhayfah ؓ was concealed amongst the enemy. Abu Sufyan announced that the Banu Qurayzah had breached the contract and did not wish to take part in the battle and so they should retreat. At the end of the meeting people hastily returned to their homes and Hudhayfah ؓ went to Prophet Muhammad ﷺ with the good news. After Prophet Muhammad ﷺ heard the news he asked for Hudhayfah ؓ to sit beside him, and upon doing so, he ﷺ placed his blanket upon Hudhayfah ؓ, and in that state he fell asleep until he was woken by Prophet Muhammad ﷺ the following morning.[186]

---

186 The details of this incident have been mentioned in *Al-Rawd al-Unuf* 3/464-465.

GHAZWAH BANU QURAYZAH

The Banu Qurayzah were proceeding to fight Prophet Muhammad ﷺ.

Type: Expedition
Date: Thursday, Dhul-Qa'dah, 5AH
Opposition: Banu Qurayzah
No. of Muslims: The companions that fought in the
                    battle of Ahzab alongside an army of
                    angels including Jibril;
                    3000 companions
No. of Unbelievers: Unknown
Outcome: Muslims gained victory

Banu Qurayzah were one of the three Jewish tribes that resided in Arabia, at the oasis of Yathrib which is now known as Madinah. It is mentioned that when the Muslims returned to Madinah after the victory of Khandaq, they laid down their weapons and released their armour. As the time of Zuhr approached, Jibrīl عليه السلام appeared before Prophet Muhammad ﷺ and questioned whether he had removed his armour. When Prophet Muhammad ﷺ affirmed, Jibrīl عليه السلام exclaimed: 'The angels have not put down their weapons yet and neither have they returned. Allah has given His

• MADINAH

Banu Qurayzah

ARABIA

Red Sea

Hunayn •

• MAKKAH

Ta'if •

orders for you to proceed towards Banu Qurayzah. For indeed I am heading in that direction too, to shake them.'[187]

Like other tribes, the Banu Qurayzah had also made a peace treaty with Prophet Muhammad ﷺ. Moreover, just like other tribes, they also breached the pact by intending to attack Madinah. In the company of an army of angels, Jibrīl عليه السلام marched towards Banu Qurayzah and so did Prophet Muhammad ﷺ with three thousand companions and thirty-six horses. Due to the large number of angels, their presence and movement clouded the entire street of Banu Ghanam.[188] Companions were instructed to head towards Banu Qurayzah and pray Asr there. This does not mean their prayer was overlooked, but it indicates their haste and the importance of reaching the location promptly.

The Muslims laid siege for fifteen days.[189] During that time, the Banu Qurayzah surrendered for they endured the terror put into them by Allah. It is mentioned that the reason for the siege lasting so long was due to the Banu Qurayzah being equipped and having a plentiful amount of food to sustain them. The chief of the Jews, named Ka'b bin Asad, conferred with his people and presented before them three options to ease their situation. He said, 'Follow this man, take this man to be truthful, for he is a messenger who is also evident in your books. For if you do, then your possessions, wives, children and wealth will be secure and protected.' The Banu Qurayzah rejected this offer as they stood firm upon their faith. Ka'b ibn Asad presented a second option to kill their children and wives and thereafter to fight against Prophet Muhammad ﷺ and the Muslims. If they were unsuccessful in battle then there would be no concern for their wives and children, and if they were victorious then they could marry and have children. The Banu Qurayzah responded to this option by saying: 'What is there to life after we kill our wives and children?' Ka'b bin Asad presented his last offer as he said: 'As you are aware, tonight is the Sabbath and the Muslims acknowledge the sacredness of this day for the Jews, hence, take this opportunity and attack

187 *Al-Rawd ul-Unuf* 3/466.
188 *Sahih Bukhari* 4118.
189 *Zarqāni* 3/73.

the Muslims whilst they are unaware and take them by surprise.'
The Banu Qurayzah (like the other two options) disregarded this
offer and exclaimed: 'Are you unaware of what happened to our
forefathers when they discredited this holy day?'[190]

The Banu Qurayzah then asked to speak to Abu Lubabah ؓ
in these challenging times. Their request was granted by Prophet
Muhammad ﷺ and Abu Lubabah ؓ presented himself before
them. Upon his entrance, the men gathered around him and the
women and children burst into tears. They asked him: 'O Abu
Lubabah, do you deem it wise for us to surrender to Muhammad
and his order?' He responded in the affirmative and he indicated with a finger to his neck that they would be killed. Whilst
Abu Lubabah ؓ remained in his seat he realised his betrayal to
Prophet Muhammad ﷺ by making the Jews aware of their plan
and so he headed towards the mosque and tied himself to a pillar,
crying that he would not be released until Allah and His Prophet
Muhammad ﷺ forgave him. He also swore not to return to the
Banu Qurayzah as it would remind him of his betrayal to Prophet
Muhammad ﷺ.

This message reached Prophet Muhammad ﷺ and he said: 'If
Abu Lubabah ؓ had come to me then I surely would have forgiven him; however, he has taken matters to Allah so now he will
have to wait for Allah's forgiveness.' Ibn Hisham mentions that
Abu Lubabah ؓ was tied for six days and was only untied by his
wife for every prayer and to relieve himself and then he would
return to his situation.[191] It is recorded that when Prophet Muhammad ﷺ was in Umm Salamah's house, Allah revealed his pardon for Abu Lubabah ؓ to Prophet Muhammad ﷺ upon which
he ﷺ smiled. Umm Salamah asked the reason for his happiness
and he revealed that Allah had forgiven Abu Lubabah and so she
requested to notify him. When she called out the good news from
her house, the companions rushed to Abu Lubabah to untie him
from his punishment; however, he refused and said: 'I have taken
an oath that I will only be untied by the blessed hands of Prophet

190 This is a summary of the incident; however, this has been mentioned in *Zarqāni*
3/64-65 and *Al-Rawd al-Unuf* 3/469.
191 The details of this incident have been recorded in *Al-Rawd al-Unuf* 3/469-471.

Muhammad ﷺ. As dawn approached and Prophet Muhammad ﷺ entered the mosque for Fajr prayer, he released Abu Lubabah from the pillar with his blessed hands.

Even though the Banu Qurayzah agreed to the decision of Prophet Muhammad ﷺ, the tribe of Aws, allies of the Banu Qurayzah against Khazraj, tried to intercede for them. Prophet Muhammad ﷺ consulted them and asked them whether they would appreciate someone from their tribe to decide what was to be done with the Banu Qurayzah. This idea was accepted and Prophet Muhammad ﷺ chose Sa'd bin Mu'az ؓ to make the judgement. When Sa'd ؓ came forth, the people gathered and pleaded for him to be sympathetic in his decision, as they were his fellow friends. Sa'd ؓ insisted that the men from the Banu Qurayzah be killed, their property be divided and for the children and women to be taken as slaves. He mentioned that he was not taking into consideration any feelings of sympathy, emotion nor the blame of anyone. The Messenger of Allah ﷺ was proud of his decision and he exclaimed, 'You have given the judgement of Allah regarding them.' It has been narrated that after Sa'd ؓ gave his verdict regarding the Banu Qurayzah, he made a supplication to Allah to allow him to live longer to fight for the cause of Allah against those who had banished Prophet Muhammad ﷺ from Makkah, but if the war had come to an end, then to take his life as a martyr. Upon his request, Sa'd's ؓ wound gushed open and blood burst out from it causing him to breathe his last.[192] Such was his love and faith that the doors of Paradise flung open to accept him and the angels rejoiced for the ascension of his soul.

---

192 The details of this narration are mentioned in *Sahih Bukhari* 4122.

GHAZWAH BANU LIHYAN

Prophet Muhammad ﷺ set out with the aim of avenging the deaths of Asim bin Thabit, Khubaib bin Adi, and other martyrs of Raj'i.

Type:	Expedition
Date:	Rabiʿ al-Awwal 6AH, 29th Safar 6AH
Opposition:	Banu Lihyan
No. of Muslims:	200 mounted warriors
No. of Unbelievers:	Unknown
Outcome:	No combat

Banu Lihyan were an Arab tribe during the time of Prophet Muhammad ﷺ and were involved in many military conflicts with him. Prophet Muhammad ﷺ intended to avenge the deaths of some great losses during the battles, namely, Asim bin Thabit ؓ, Khubaib bin Adi ؓ, and a few others (may they rest in peace).

On the first of Rabiʿ al-Awwal 6AH, with an army of two hundred mounted warriors, Prophet Muhammad ﷺ set out towards the residence of Banu Lihyan. He ﷺ first took the route towards Syria and thereafter towards Māhis, which is a valley to the west of Madinah, approximately 15km on the road to Syria from Madinah. He ﷺ later went from Batra to a place in the west of Madinah until they reached Ghuran, the area where the

ARABIA

Banu Lihyan

• Hunayn

• MAKKAH

• Hudaybiyah

Ta'if •

Red Sea

companions gained martyrdom.[193] As soon as the Banu Lihyan sensed the presence of Prophet Muhammad ﷺ, they scattered and took refuge in the mountains. Prophet Muhammad ﷺ camped in the area for one to two days.[194] During his stay he sent out a small group in search of members of the Banu Lihyan. Amidst all the groups, one consisted of ten men led by Abu Bakr ؓ.[195]

With no battles to fight, Prophet Muhammad ﷺ returned home to Madinah. On his journey back he reiterated a few words. 'We are returning, we are repenting, we are submissive to our Lord, and praising Him. We seek refuge in Allah from the difficulties of this journey, from a gloomy return and a displeasing sight regarding our family and wealth.'[196]

193 *Al-Rawd al-Unuf* 3/525-526.
194 *Zarqāni* 3/107.
195 Ibid, p.108.
196 *Al-Rawd al-Unuf* 3/526.

GHAZWAH DHI-QARAD

*Abu Dharr's son, who was appointed to guard the camels, was
killed in the raid and Abu Dharr's wife was kidnapped.*

Type:	Expedition
Date:	12th Rabi' al-Awwal 6AH
Opposition:	Uyaynah bin Hisn Fazari
No. of Muslims:	500 or 700 men
Losses:	4
No. of Unbelievers:	40 mounted horsemen
Losses:	4
Outcome:	Muslims defeated the polytheists. Prophet Muhammad ﷺ spent night and day in the location and performed Salahtul-khawf there as well. After five days he returned to Madinah.

Dhi Qarad is the name of a water spring situated in the vicinity of Ghatafan.[197] This area was also considered to be the grazing land of Prophet Muhammad's ﷺ camels. This event transpired in Rabi' al-Awwal 6AH, before Khaybar, and some are of the view that it was before Hudaybiyah.[198]

197 *Fath ul-Bari* 7/574.
198 *Zarqāni* 3/109.

• Buwat

Dhi-Qarad

MADINAH •

• Safwan

ARABIA

• Badr

The battle arose as a consequence of the actions of Uyaynah bin Hisn Fazari. In the company of forty mounted horsemen, he raided the meadow of Prophet Muhammad's ﷺ camels. After doing so, he fled with all the camels. In the process of this siege Abu Dharr's son, who was appointed to guard the camels, was killed, and his mother, the wife of Abu Dharr, was abducted.

As soon as the word spread, Salmah bin Akwa' set out in pursuit of help. From the heights of the hillock, he projected his voice and called out 'O companions' thrice. The call for help alerted the companions and echoed through Madinah. Salmah bin Akwa' was a well-known archer, and with his skills and talent, he traced the location of Uyaynah bin Hisn and the herd of camels. The tracks led him to a nearby water spring called Dhi Qarad. Salmah bin Akwa' struck his arrows whilst chanting: 'I am the son of Akwa'. This day will distinguish who drank the milk of a noble woman and a cowardly woman.'[199] He scaffolded the enemies from all areas until he was able to release all the camels, also managing to collect thirty garments.[200]

Five hundred or seven hundred soldiers of Prophet Muhammad ﷺ marched through the land with speed and urgency.[201] Prophet Muhammad ﷺ released a small group of warriors in advance. This small group engaged with the enemy from the moment of their arrival. Two lives were lost from the opposition and one from the Muslim army: Mas'adah bin Hakamah, who was killed by Abu Qatada ؓ, and Aban bin Umar, who was killed by Ukkashah bin Mihsan ؓ. The Muslims lost Muhriz bin Nadlah ؓ who was also known as Akhram; he was martyred by Abdur Rahman bin Uyaynah.[202] Salmah bin Akwa' ؓ confronted Prophet Muhammad ﷺ and exclaimed: 'O Prophet Muhammad ﷺ! I have stopped the people from drinking water and now they are thirsty. So send after them at this time.' Upon this Prophet Muhammad ﷺ replied: 'O Ibn ul-Akwa'! Now that you have overpowered

---

199 Ibid, p.116.
200 *Sahih Bukhari* 4194.
201 *Zarqāni* 3/113.
202 Ibid p.114, *Al-Rawd al-Unuf* 4/9.

them, show mercy.'[203] The disbelievers took flight upon their defeat. Prophet Muhammad ﷺ stayed put in the location for one night and day. Thereafter, he performed Salahtul-Khawf (prayer of fear), and after five days elapsed he returned to Madinah.[204]

203 *Fath ul-Bari* 7/353, *Sahih al-Bukhari* 4194.
204 *Zarqāni* 3/119.

UMRATUL-HUDAYBIYAH

Prophet Muhammad ﷺ and his companions set out to Makkah to perform umrah. They did not have the intention for combat, therefore, they were not equipped.

Type:	Expedition
Date:	Monday 1st Dhul-Qa'dah (6AH)
	End of Shawwal 6AH
Opposition:	Quraysh
No. of Muslims:	1500 Muhajirun and Ansar
No. of Unbelievers:	Unknown
Outcome:	The peace treaty of Hudaybiyah:

The peace treaty of Hudaybiyah:
All hostilities will cease for the next ten years.
Any member of the Quraysh who flees to Madinah without permission of his master or guardian will be returned even though he is a Muslim.
Any Muslims that travel to Makkah from Madinah will not be returned to the Muslims.
There will be no fights or treachery during this time.
Prophet Muhammad ﷺ was not allowed to perform umrah this year but allowed to enter Makkah the following year for three days.
The other tribes have the option to ally themselves to any group they wish.

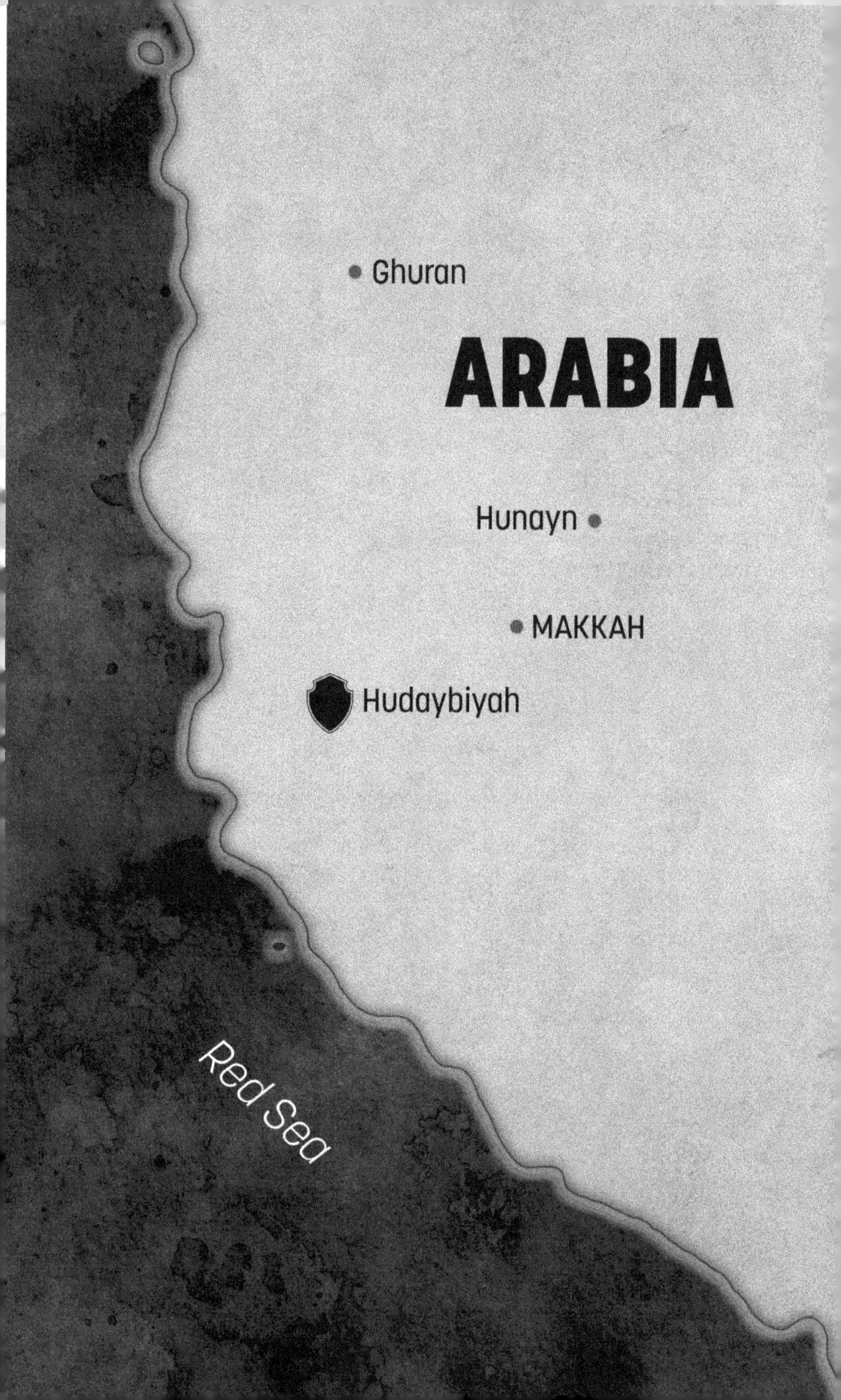
Ghuran
ARABIA
Hunayn
MAKKAH
Hudaybiyah
Red Sea

Hudaybiyah is the name of a well situated in a village, and due to the well the village also became known as Hudaybiyah. Others have said it is the name of a tree there approximately nine miles from Makkah. Muhib Tabari says: 'The majority of Hudaybiyah is connected to the al-Haram[205] and the rest is in the hill area.'[206]

Prophet Muhammad ﷺ dreamt that he entered Makkah accompanied by a few of his companions. It was calm and tranquil as they partook in the activities of umrah.[207] Some companions had completed *halq*[208] whilst others had just trimmed their hair.[209] Prophet Muhammad ﷺ awoke from this vivid dream and narrated it to his companions; it rejuvenated their spirit.

On Monday 1st Dhul-Qa'dah 6AH, Prophet Muhammad ﷺ set out from Madinah accompanied by fourteen hundred Muhajirūn and Ansār,[210] with the intention of performing umrah. As soon as they reached a place called Dhul Hulayfah, the Muslims secured their camels and made *ish'ar*.[211] After donning their ihrams, Prophet Muhammad ﷺ despatched Busr bin Sufyan ؓ to spy on the Quraysh and their incoming movements. They carried no weapons with them; their sole purpose was to perform umrah. When Prophet Muhammad ﷺ arrived at Ghadir Ashtat, they were informed that the Quraysh had started to amass an army upon hearing of Prophet Muhammad's ﷺ arrival. They were also notified that they intended to fight and were committed to not allowing Prophet Muhammad ﷺ enter Makkah.[212]

Prophet Muhammad ﷺ continued his journey until he reached a place called Hudaybiyah. He pitched camp although there was less water. Due to the severity of the heat, people started to complain to him. He handed them an arrow and told them to insert

---

205 Masjid al-Haram, where the Ka'bah is situated.
206 *Zarqāni* 3/169-170.
207 Smaller pilgrimage to Makkah.
208 Shaving of the head in order to come out of the state of Ihraam.
209 Ibid.
210 Ibid.
211 Ish'ar is a reference to a small mark on the camels so that they can be determined amongst the rest. *Zarqāni* 3/173.
212 Ibid p.174.

it into the waterhole. Water started gushing forth from the hole, enough for everyone to quench their thirst with.[213]

On behalf of the Muslims, Prophet Muhammad ﷺ sent Uthman bin Affan ؓ as the spokesperson. Prophet Muhammad ﷺ told him to inform the believing women and men of Makkah that they no longer had to conceal their religion. He also mentioned that the Muslims were there to only perform umrah and had no intention of fighting.[214] Uthman bin Affan ؓ entered Makkah and did what he was commanded to. After completing his speech, the Quraysh said, 'If you would like to perform *tawaf* of the Ka'bah, then we will allow you to do so.' Uthman bin Affan ؓ replied, 'I will not perform *tawaf* until Prophet Muhammad ﷺ has completed his.' Rumour spread of the death of Uthman bin Affan ؓ, resulting in havoc and dismay. Under an acacia tree, the pledge was taken[215] to fight till the last man stands. Later, the Muslims heard that Uthman bin Affan ؓ was alive. Four more envoys were sent to the Quraysh, but they stayed firm and stuck to their word.

Approaching from a distance, Suhayl bin Amr, acting as the spokesperson for Quraysh, came to Prophet Muhammad ﷺ. It was during this meeting that the treaty of Hudaybiyah was formulated, and the following points were agreed upon:

- Firstly, the Muslims would return the following year to perform umrah.
- Secondly, if any man among the Quraysh went to Madinah and accepted Islam, he would be returned to Makkah. However, if any of the Muslims went to Makkah they would not be returned.
- Thirdly, war would be abstained from for ten years; there would only be peace and tranquility.
- Lastly, whoever wanted to enter an alliance with Muhammad could do so, and anyone who wanted to enter an alliance with the Quraysh could do so.[216]

---

213 Ibid pp.180-181.
214 *Al-Rahīq ul-Makhtūm* p.292.
215 Bay'at Ridwān.
216 Ibid p.293.

Disheartened as they were, the companions and Prophet Muhammad ﷺ returned to Madinah without performing umrah after spending ten days near Hudaybiyah.[217] When Umar ؓ asked Prophet Muhammad ﷺ if this was a clear victory, he replied 'Yes.' Shortly after Prophet Muhammad ﷺ returned to Madinah, a man named Abu Basir fled from Makkah to be with him, but he was later returned according to the treaty.[218] However, on the coast, he fled again, and this time, he was joined by Suhayl. The number of individuals in their group increased to seventy. They set themselves up on a trade route, ambushing Makkan caravans returning from Syria and taking all their goods. Within a year, many of the idol-worshippers had embraced Islam. The Quraysh leaders sent a message to Prophet Muhammad ﷺ, requesting him to keep the people in Madinah and not send them back to Makkah. The treaty of Hudaybiyah improved the relationship between the Muslims and non-Muslims.

217 Ibid p.228.
218 Ibid p.297.

GHAZWAH AL-KHAYBAR

The Jews resided in a land which had fortresses. They betrayed the Muslims by enticing the disbelievers against the Muslims in Khandaq. This battle teaches us to strike a balance between this world and the hereafter. This world should be a means for the ultimate success in the hereafter.

Type:	Expedition
Date:	End of Muharram, 7AH
Opposition:	Jews of Khaybar
	Banu Nadir and the Banu Qurayzah
No. of Muslims:	1,400 infantry and 400 cavalry
Losses:	Less than 20 and 50 wounded
No. of Unbelievers:	10,000
Losses:	93
Outcome:	Muslims gained victory

Khaybar is a large city that consists of fortresses and agricultural lands, some distance from Madinah in the direction of Syria.[219] Al-Baqri mentions this to be the name of a man from the people of Egypt, whose name was Khaybar bin Qaniyah bin Mahlayila.[220] It was a Jewish colony with fortresses and considered the headquarters of the Jewish troops. Khaybar was the last

219 *Zarqāni* 3/243.
220 *Al-Rawd al-Unuf* 4/72.

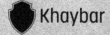 Khaybar

ARABIA

• Uhud

• MADINAH

and strongest of Jewish forts in Arabia.[221] Prophet Muhammad ﷺ wanted to be secure from the instigations of the Jews, as they spent much of their wealth on stirring up hatred and inciting neighbouring Arab tribes to fight against Prophet Muhammad ﷺ in Khandaq.

After returning from Hudaybiyah, Prophet Muhammad ﷺ stayed in Madinah for the month of Dhul-Hijjah and a part of Muharram.[222] At the end of Muharram, with an army of fourteen hundred men and two hundred horses, Prophet Muhammad ﷺ set out for Khaybar.[223] Those who were weak and frivolous at Hudaybiyah were restricted from accompanying in Khaybar. A total of twenty women also accompanied the Muslim army to aid the wounded and sick. It was the norm for Prophet Muhammad ﷺ to attack in the morning and not at night. If he ﷺ heard the call of *adhan* in the morning he would not attack as it was a sign of believers existing in that area; however, if there was no sound of *adhan* then Prophet Muhammad ﷺ would command to attack.[224]

As the morning approached, Prophet Muhammad ﷺ headed towards Khaybar with his army. When the early morning labourers laid their eyes on Prophet Muhammad ﷺ, they cried out, 'Muhammad is here with his *khamis*.'[225] *Khamis* comes from the words *khams* which means five; the Jews indicated that Prophet Muhammad ﷺ was there with his whole army, since an army is divided into five sections: the vanguard, the right-wing, the left-wing, the mainstay, and finally the rear guard.[226] The Messenger of Allah ﷺ and his army overpowered the fortresses of Khaybar, starting with the fort of Naʻim. The Jews were well-prepared as they enclosed themselves in their forts. Prophet Muhammad ﷺ sent Abu Bakr ؓ and thereafter Umar ؓ to conquer the fort; however, they were unsuccessful.

Prophet Muhammad ﷺ said, 'Tomorrow I will hand over this flag to someone who loves Allah and His Messenger and they love

221 *Qasas un-Nabiyeen*, p.234.
222 *Al-Rawd al-Unuf* 4/72.
223 *Zarqāni* 3/245.
224 Ibid p.252.
225 Ibid pp.252-253.
226 Ibid p.254.

him likewise.' The day after, Prophet Muhammad ﷺ summoned Ali ؓ who had ophthalmia at the time. He ﷺ cured his eyes with his blessed saliva. Ali ؓ was advised by Prophet Muhammad ﷺ to first invite the Jews to Islam and to enlighten their hearts thereafter, and if they disagreed, then to attack.[227] The prophecy materialised and Ali ؓ conquered the fort of Na'im. It is mentioned that when Ali ؓ came near the fort, Mahrab, a well-known Jewish warrior, confronted Ali ؓ, glorifying his bravery and excellence. Immediately, they began the one-to-one combat. Ali ؓ took the final blow and struck through the helmet of Mahrab, causing his head to split in half.[228] Thereafter, Al-Hubab ibn Mundhir took charge of attacking As-Sa'b fort and he remained there for three days, after which the Muslims gained victory.[229]

Soon after, the Jews evacuated An-Natāt and rushed into Az-Zubair fort, where they felt protected due to it being barred. A Jewish spy advised Prophet Muhammad ﷺ to stop the water supply of the Jews as this would provoke them to fight the Muslims. The water supply was cut off and just as anticipated, the Jews were forced to react. When they left their fort they fought the Muslims and as a result, ten Jews were killed and the fort was conquered.[230] The Jews fled the fort and found safety in another called Abi castle. Here they remained for three days before Abu Dujanah ؓ barged into the fort and conquered the castle.[231]

Lastly, the Jews barricaded themselves in An-Nizar fort, which was considered to be the strongest and best fortified. After locking themselves away, they lobbed arrows and threw stones at the Muslims yet were too cowardly to fight in person. However, the Muslims gained victory and the Jews fled in all directions, leaving the children and women abandoned.[232]

The second siege of Khaybar lasted for fourteen days. Prophet Muhammad ﷺ swiftly moved towards Al-Katiba where he conquered

---

227 Ibid pp.256-257.
228 *Al-Rawd al-Unuf* 4/80.
229 *Al-Rahīq ul-Makhtūm* p.317.
230 Ibid p.318.
231 Ibid.
232 Ibid.

the remaining forts with peace negotiations.[233] When the Jews gathered to attack the Muslims, this caught the attention of an Abyssinian slave who was grazing his master's sheep. The Jews proclaimed that they intended to kill Prophet Muhammad ﷺ, who claimed to be a Prophet. This slave went directly to Prophet Muhammad ﷺ to converse with him. He asked who he was and what the religion of Islam had to offer. Prophet Muhammad ﷺ replied, 'You have to testify that there is no god but Allah and I am Prophet Muhammad, the Messenger of Allah. By accepting this and dying with this faith you will enter Paradise.' The Abyssinian slave instantly accepted Islam. He later sought advice from Prophet Muhammad ﷺ on what to do with his master's flock. He ﷺ advised him to leave the sheep near the fort and by the will of Allah, they would find their master.[234]

Later, a bedouin also came into the fold of Islam. When he was given a share of the booty he brought it back to return to Prophet Muhammad ﷺ. This left everyone in amazement. He explained his intention: the bedouin accepted Islam so that he could be martyred in the path of Allah and thereby gain entrance to Paradise. He did not long for or desire anything else when accepting Islam. Both of these courageous souls were later martyred on the battlefield. Allah accepted their wish and raised their souls to the sky. May Allah have mercy on them.

When all hope was gone, the Jews agreed on a peace treaty. They were offered a deal, which included them providing half of the fruits and produce of Khaybar to Madinah annually. They agreed to this. Every year, Abdullah bin Rawahah ؓ would visit Khaybar to obtain half the produce, but the Jews were always given the option to keep what they wished.[235]

During this battle, many events transpired. Zainab bint Al-Harith, the wife of Sallam ibn Mikhsham, presented poisoned meat to the Prophet Muhammad ﷺ. Upon placing the meat in his mouth, Prophet Muhammad ﷺ realised its condition and spat it out. He called for the Jews and asked them about the situation.

233 Ibid p.319.
234 The details of this incident are mentioned in *Qasas un-Nabiyeen* 5/239-240.
235 *Al-Rahīq ul-Makhtūm* pp.320-321.

They were truthful and declared their intentions to kill Prophet Muhammad ﷺ. In their defence, they explained that they were eager to see whether he was a genuine prophet or not. If he was, the poison would not affect him and if it did, then they could conclude that he is false. Prophet Muhammad ﷺ was not afflicted by this poison; however, a companion who did eat the meat passed away. As a result, Zainab faced the penalty of death.[236] However, there are different opinions as to what happened to her; some say that she was pardoned.

Along the way, three other lands were also conquered: Fadaq, Wadi Qurra, and Tayma'a, the residents of which agreed to a peace treaty with Prophet Muhammad ﷺ. A significant amount of booty was gained; however, the lands of the Jews were still under their authority and left for them. After the earnest actions of the companions during Hudaybiyah, Allah had planned a great victory for the Muslims. The large amount of booty that was gained from Khaybar was shared amongst the companions.[237] This was a victory bestowed upon them by Allah.

---

236 Ibid pp.322-323.

237 The details of how much they received is mentioned in *Al-Rahīq ul-Makhtūm* pp.320-321.

FATHU MAKKAH

*A peace treaty was signed between Prophet Muhammad ﷺ
and the Quraysh, with the condition that the other two parties,
the tribes of Banu Bakr and Banu Khuza'ah, were given the
chance to join. Abu Sufyan left Makkah in order to renew the
peace treaty as it was broken by the Quraysh, as they denied
paying the blood money or the other options given by Prophet
Muhammad ﷺ. During this incident one of the staunch enemies
of Islam, Abu Sufyan, accepts Islam. This battle teaches us the
quality of forgiveness and how Prophet Muhammad ﷺ, rather
than ordering Abu Sufyan to be executed, invited him to Islam.*

Type:	Expedition
Date:	10th Ramadan, 8AH
Opposition:	Quraysh
No. of Muslims:	10,000
Losses:	2
No. of Unbelievers:	Unknown
Losses:	12
Outcome:	Muslims are given the permission to enter Makkah.

As time passed, Islam became the leading religion spreading rapidly across the Arabian Peninsula. Allah directed Prophet Muhammad ﷺ and his community of Muslims to enter Makkah. They would cleanse the Ka'bah by demolishing and removing all three hundred and sixty idols and images within and surrounding

Waddan

ARABIA

MAKKAH

Hudaybiyah

Ta'if

Red Sea

the Ka'bah, so that it could become known as the pivotal point of guidance for the whole of mankind. Makkah's sacred status would be restored and the city would regain its true purpose.

From the treaty of Hudaybiyah, we come to know that the Quraysh signed a peace treaty with Prophet Muhammad ﷺ in which one of the key conditions was that alliances could be formed freely between the parties and other tribes. Therefore whosoever chose to enter an alliance with Muhammad ﷺ was free to do so. Likewise, whoever desired to enter an alliance with the Quraysh was free to do so.[238]

The Banu Bakr allied with the Quraysh, while their bitter enemies, the Banu Khuza'ah, allied with Muhammad ﷺ. This treaty enabled both parties to bring peace between themselves. However, soon after, an incident transpired in which the Banu Bakr attacked the Banu Khuza'ah by night, causing the death of twelve of their men. The Banu Bakr were aided by the Quraysh with weapons to carry out this treacherous task.[239]

In search for help, Amr ibn Salim al-Khuza'i went to the Messenger of Allah ﷺ and related the incident. He claimed that the Quraysh had violated the pact; they had attacked some of his men whilst they were occupied in prayer. Muhammad ﷺ assured him of aid. A message was sent to the Quraysh, requesting them to compensate for their ill-treatment and to accept one of three conditions. It was imperative for them to either accept paying the blood money to the victims of Banu Khuza'ah, to end their alliance with the Banu Bakr, or to consider the treaty to be nullified. They replied with arrogance and disregarded the consequences.[240]

Soon after, Amr ibn Salim al-Khuza'i returned with news of Banu Bakr's negligence towards Prophet Muhammad's ﷺ offer. With the insight he possessed, Muhammad ﷺ mentioned to the companions to expect Abu Sufyan to come and discuss matters of the pact soon. At the behest of his people, Abu Sufyan arrived to clarify matters with Prophet Muhammad ﷺ concerning the pact.

238 *Zarqāni* 3/377.
239 Ibid p.378-379.
240 *Al-Rahīq ul-Makhtūm* p.339.

Abu Sufyan sought the help of his daughter Umm Habiba
🙏 was married to the Prophet 🕌. As he entered his daughter's
home and proceeded to sit on Prophet Muhammad's 🕌 carpet,
she instantly started to roll up the mat. Upon this sudden reaction, Abu Sufyan remarked, 'I am unsure as to why you do this? Is
it because the carpet is too good for me or that I am too good for
the carpet?' His daughter's response left him dumbfounded. She,
the wife of Prophet Muhammad 🕌, replied, 'This carpet belongs
to the Prophet Muhammad 🕌 and you are an unclean disbeliever.'
Distraught, Abu Sufyan later addressed this issue to Muhammad
🕌 but received no reply. He then went to Abu Bakr 🙏 to ask him
to speak with Prophet Muhammad 🕌, but he refused. He later
tried to convince Umar 🙏, Ali 🙏, to aid him in the matter; all
refused to speak on his behalf. They also proclaimed the matter to
be serious and requested to not be involved. Abu Sufyan was left
baffled and confused as to what approach to take next.[241]

On the third day, Amr ibn Salim marched towards Madinah
with forty horsemen to address the Prophet Muhammad 🕌 regarding Banu Bakr's treachery and to seek help for revenge.[242]
Prophet Muhammad 🕌 sent out eight soldiers under the command of Qatādah bin Rabi' to Edam, a short distance from Madinah, to divert the attention of the people from the main attack. It
was during this sensitive time that Hātib bin Abi Balta'ah wrote
a letter to the Quraysh, warning them of the unexpected attack.
Prophet Muhammad 🕌 received revelation regarding this matter.
Hātib sent a woman named Z'ama Muhammad bin Ja'far to de-
liver the letter, which was discreetly hidden in her hair. Prophet
Muhammad 🕌 immediately sent Ali 🙏 and Zubair bin Awwam 🙏
to stop the woman and to retrieve the letter. After she was caught
and the letter was taken, Hātib confessed to his actions and apol-
ogised to the Prophet Muhammad 🕌. Hātib clarified his actions
were not due to enmity against Islam or the Prophet Muhammad 🕌, but rather to protect his family who were still present in
Makkah. Prophet Muhammad 🕌 heard his apology and accepted

241 Ibid p.340-341.
242 *Zarqāni* 3/380.

it; however, Umar ﷺ wanted to 'strike off his head', upon which Prophet Muhammad ﷺ said, 'O Umar, he is a companion of Badr and Allah is likely to favour the companions of Badr.'[243]

Prophet Muhammad ﷺ secretly prepared for battle against the Quraysh. He wanted to take them by surprise, so with an army of ten thousand men, Prophet Muhammad ﷺ marched towards Makkah. Upon reaching al-Qaded, the Muslims ended their fast with the available water and thereafter marched to a location called Marr uz-Zahran and camped there. By the power of Allah, the emergence of the Muslim army in Makkah was still concealed.[244]

The Prophet ﷺ wanted to avoid to avoid catching the Quraysh off guard, so he ordered his men to light fires for cooking, allowing them to assess the situation accurately. Umar bin Al-Khattab was assigned guard duty, while Abu Sufyan, along with two polytheists, Hakim bin Hizam and Budail bin Warqua', went out for reconnaissance. Abu Sufyan requested Al-Abbas bin Abdul Muttalib to accompany him to Prophet Muhammad's ﷺ camp, in fear of being attacked. Soon after Abu Sufyan arrived, the conversation became heated. Despite the fact that Abu Sufyan now acknowledged and believed in the good traits of Prophet Muhammad ﷺ, he still denied him to be the Messenger of Allah. Al-Abbas intervened and made a rather bold demand of him: to accept Islam, or suffer. It was the will of Allah and the fate of Abu Sufyan that he accepted Islam at that moment, in the camp of Muhammad ﷺ, during Ramadan 8AH.[245]

It was decided and announced that no one would be harmed. Whoever sought refuge in the mosque would be safe, whoever sought refuge in the house of Abu Sufyan would be safe and those who wished to stay at home would be granted their request.[246] On Tuesday the 17th of Ramadan, Prophet Muhammad ﷺ left Marr uz-Zahran and upon his leave, Prophet Muhammad ﷺ commanded Abbas ﷺ to showcase the great army of Muslims marching

243 *Al-Rawd al-Unuf* 4/161-163.
244 *Al-Rahīq ul-Makhtūm* p.343.
245 Ibid pp.344-345.
246 Ibid.

towards Makkah. As Abu Sufyan laid his eyes on the army marching towards Makkah, he asked Abbas ﷺ who they were. Abbas ﷺ
replied they were the valiant warriors of Prophet Muhammad ﷺ
heading towards Makkah, to which Abu Sufyan said, 'No army
can resist the powerful army of Prophet Muhammad ﷺ.' He added, 'The power of your brother's son cannot overpower.' Abbas
ﷺ corrected his statement and said, 'Rather, it is the power of
prophethood.' Abu Sufyan affirmed this statement.[247]

It was a Friday morning in Ramadan when Prophet Muhammad ﷺ and the Muslim community entered Makkah. It was a
day of joy and accomplishment. Prophet Muhammad ﷺ entered
Makkah with a black turban wrapped around his head[248] and
with his head bowed in gratitude and humility before Allah. As he
entered with his head bowed, he ﷺ glorified Allah the Most High
for the conquest.[249] Usamah bin Zayd rode behind him, a freed
slave, demonstrating Islam's emphasis on justice and equality.[250]
Prophet Muhammad ﷺ described the day of the Conquest of
Makkah as a day of 'mercy and forgiveness, when Allah will exalt
the Quraysh and raise the honour for the Ka'bah.'

A small confrontation occurred. Safwan ibn Umayyah, Ikrimah bin Abi Jahl and Suhayl bin Amr attacked the troop of Khalid bin Walid. In defence, twelve of the Quraysh members were
killed. Prophet Muhammad ﷺ said that only in defence could one
attack on this auspicious day.[251]

Prophet Muhammad ﷺ appointed Khalid bin Walid ﷺ to enter Makkah from its lower routes with other companions. He
ﷺ commanded Zubair bin Awwam ﷺ to enter the city from the
upper side, holding the banner of Prophet Muhammad ﷺ, and for
Abu Ubaidah ﷺ to use the side valley.[252] After performing *tawaf*
of the Ka'bah, Prophet Muhammad ﷺ purified it by removing
all idols and images of gods.[253] He called upon the key holder.

247 Ibid.
248 *Sunan an-Nasa'i* 5344.
249 *Al-Rawd al-Unuf* 4/171.
250 *Sahih Bukhari* 4289.
251 *Al-Rahiq ul-Makhtum* p.347.
252 *Al-Rawd al-Unuf* 4/175, *Al-Rahiq ul-Makhtum* p.346.
253 *Al-Rawd al-Unuf* 4/183.

As the door was unlocked, he conveyed to the Banu Talha, 'Take responsibility in taking care of the house of Allah till the Day of Judgement. None will take this key away from you but a tyrant.'[254] Prophet Muhammad ﷺ called for Uthman bin Abi Shaybah ؓ, who had not yet accepted Islam, and placed the key in his hands. He reminded him that the key had been in his lineage since the beginning, and would remain so until and unless it was taken from him by a tyrant.

For the first time, the *adhan* was proclaimed openly in Makkah, with no discrimination or restrictions. As Bilal ؓ delivered the call to prayer on the roof of the Ka'bah, the words echoed around the entire city.[255] Muhammad ﷺ bathed in the house of Umm Hani. Later, he performed eight units of Salah-tul-Duha[256] to glorify and thank Allah for the conquest.[257] Amidst the peace and harmony, Fatima bint Makhzum committed an act of theft. Usama bin Zayd sought mercy for his sister. Prophet Muhammad ﷺ emphasised the impact of stealing, and how if his daughter were to steal then she would also bear the consequences of *hadd* (penalty).

It was a day of victory, a day of peace. People in large numbers gathered on Mount Safa to embrace the faith of Islam. First, the men came to pledge allegiance and then the women. Amongst the swathes of people was Hind, the wife of Abu Sufyan. She beseeched Prophet Muhammad ﷺ to pardon her for her past so that she could begin with a clean slate, and her request was granted.[258]

It was an emotional moment for Prophet Muhammad ﷺ to return to his hometown and birthplace. Many of the Ansār presumed Prophet Muhammad ﷺ would not return to Madinah due to the conquest of Makkah. Prophet Muhammad ﷺ reassured them that, 'I seek refuge with Allah. I will live with you and I will die with you.'[259]

---

254 *Tarīkh-e-Makkah tul-Mukaramah wa Masjid al-Haram* p.62.
255 *Al-Rahīq ul-Makhtūm* p.348.
256 Optional prayer that can be prayed from sunrise to midday.
257 *Al-Rawd al-Unuf* 4/182.
258 *Al-Rahīq ul-Makhtūm* p.351.
259 Ibid.

As the Muslims assembled in Makkah, Prophet Muhammad ﷺ proclaimed that this city would remain a sanctuary forever. He remained in Makkah for nineteen days[260] and during his stay, he ﷺ forbade the spilling of blood and the cutting of trees in the city.[261] It was not lawful for anyone before him and neither for anyone after. Sooner or later, the impact of the Conquest of Makkah became evident. People came in large numbers to accept Islam, and the religion spread far across Arabia.[262]

260 Ibid p.352.
261 Ibid p.350.
262 Surah Nasr.

GHAZWAH AL-HUNAYN

*The Banu Hawazin and Thaqif thought that after the conquest
of Makkah Prophet Muhammad ﷺ would attack them, so they
prepared to fight the Muslims. This battle teaches us that victory
comes from Allah regardless of the number of men in the army.*

Type:	Battle
Date:	6th or 8th of Shawwal, 8AH
Opposition:	Banu Hawazin and Thaqif
No. of Muslims:	12,000 men
Losses:	Unknown
No. of Unbelievers:	20,000 men
Losses:	70
Outcome:	Muslims gained victory

Hunayn, also known as Hawazin, is the name of a place approximately twenty-six kilometers from the east of Makkah.[263] Hunayn is possibly also named after Hunayn bin Qaniyah bin Mihlayil, as mentioned by Ibn Hisham.[264] However, others have said it is a valley near Zi Majaz[265] north of Ta'if.[266] This very place between Makkah and Ta'if is where the Banu Hawazin and Thaqif resided. After the Conquest of Makkah it occurred to these tribes

---

263 *Al-Rawd al-Unuf* 4/218.
264 Ibid.
265 Name of a market.
266 *Zarqāni* 3/496.

Badr

ARABIA

Ghuran

Hunayn

MAKKAH

Hudaybiyah

Red Sea

that they may be the next targets of Prophet Muhammad ﷺ. Thus, after some deliberation they decided to attack Madinah.

They left with an army of twenty thousand warriors with Malik bin Auf Nasri as their chief.[267] Malik advised his well-equipped warriors to bring their wives and children believing they would provide courage and support while discouraging them from fleeing the battle.[268] Despite his old age, the wise Duraid bin Summah joined the warriors. Upon reaching a location called Awtās, Duraid advised the army to settle down in the area as it was an appropriate land for battle. Soon after, a commotion arose, with children crying and donkeys braying. After seeing such a spectacle, Duraid was not confident with Malik's idea of bringing their families to battle with them as a means of encouragement; he explained how it would be humiliating for their families if they were defeated. Malik was adamant and said, 'If my decision is not obeyed, then I shall give my life.' Fearing the loss of their leader, all the warriors pledged their allegiance and acceptance of his decision.[269]

Abdullah bin Abi Hadr ؓ was sent as a spy by Prophet Muhammad ﷺ to the opposition party for information and to discover their whereabouts. Abdullah sat amongst the army of Malik and later returned to narrate the situation to Prophet Muhammad ﷺ. Prophet Muhammad ﷺ then began preparations for war.[270]

It was the 8th of Shawwal 8AH when Prophet Muhammad ﷺ left for battle. He marched through the land with an army of twelve thousand,[271] and also eighty participants from the disbelievers; amongst them was Safwan bin Umayyah from whom Prophet Muhammad ﷺ borrowed a hundred pieces of armour.[272] From the crowd, a voice called out, 'Today we will not be defeated because of small numbers.' This remark reflected the pride within their hearts, yet the cloak of pride can only be worn by Allah.

---

267 Ibid p.497.
268 *Al-Rahīq ul-Makhtūm* p.355.
269 *Al-Rawd al-Unuf* 4/218-220.
270 Ibid p.221.
271 *Zarqāni* 3/498.
272 Ibid p.499.

This was not pleasing to Allah, hence, they were later tested in the battle.[273]

Upon the Muslim army's arrival at the valley of Hunayn, the Hawazin and Thaqif were already poised for an attack. Malik devised a strategy for all twenty thousand warriors to strike simultaneously as soon as the Muslims entered the area. This surprise attack caught the Muslims off guard, resulting in a sudden shock and causing the majority to scatter.

This left ten companions[274] surrounding Prophet Muhammad ﷺ. Upon this, Prophet Muhammad ﷺ turned to his right and called out, 'Where are you, O people? Come towards me! I am the messenger of Allah and I am the grandson of Abdul Mutalib.'[275] However, the Prophet's voice was drowned out by the din of battle but Abbas bin Abdul Muttalib possessed a very loud voice. Projecting his voice as far it could reach, he exclaimed, 'O people of the Ansār! O those who had pledged their allegiance under the acacia tree.'[276] Instantly, the Muslims gathered around Prophet Muhammad ﷺ, denoting their presence by chanting *Labbaik Labbaik* (I am present) and charged to attack. As the battle intensified, Prophet Muhammad ﷺ took a handful of sand and read upon it the following, 'May your faces be disgraced.'[277] There was not a single person whom the sand did not reach, resulting in the opposition to either flee the battlefield or be captured.[278] Upon this incident, Allah revealed the following verses in Surah Tawbah:

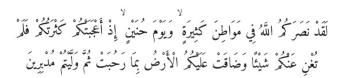

لَقَدْ نَصَرَكُمُ اللّٰهُ فِي مَوَاطِنَ كَثِيرَةٍ وَيَوْمَ حُنَيْنٍ إِذْ أَعْجَبَتْكُمْ كَثْرَتُكُمْ فَلَمْ تُغْنِ عَنكُمْ شَيْئًا وَضَاقَتْ عَلَيْكُمُ الْأَرْضُ بِمَا رَحُبَتْ ثُمَّ وَلَّيْتُم مُّدْبِرِينَ

273 *Al-Rahīq ul-Makhtūm* p.357.
274 *Al-Rawd al-Unuf* p.226.
275 Ibid p.225.
276 Ibid p.228.
277 *Al-Rahīq ul-Makhtūm* p.358.
278 Ibid.

Indeed, Allah has made you successful in many battles, and even on Hunayn, when you were proud of your great number and they proved of no help whatsoever to you, for the earth, despite all its vastness, became narrow for you and you turned back, retreating.[279]

$$\text{ثُمَّ أَنْزَلَ اللَّهُ سَكِينَتَهُ عَلَى رَسُولِهِ وَعَلَى الْمُؤْمِنِينَ وَأَنْزَلَ جُنُودًا لَمْ تَرَوْهَا}$$

$$\text{وَعَذَّبَ الَّذِينَ كَفَرُوا ۚ وَذَلِكَ جَزَاءُ الْكَافِرِينَ}$$

Then Allah sent His peace upon His Messenger and upon the believers, and bestowed upon you forces which you could not see, and punished those who disbelieved and that is the recompense for those who disbelieve.[280]

In the narration by Jubair bin Mut'im, he describes witnessing a peculiar phenomenon before the people were defeated. He saw that something descended from the sky, resembling a black cloak, which separated the people and dispersed like ants, filling up the valley. 'I did not doubt that it was angels, then I witnessed the people being defeated.'[281] A lesson to be extracted from this battle is that numbers do not win a battle. It is the tactics and faith that one has in their religion, and ultimately their reliance on Allah.

After their defeat, the opposition dispersed into different localities; some went towards Awtās, others towards Ta'if, and some towards Nakhla.[282] A group was sent with Abu Amir to catch up with some of the escapists and as a result, Abu Amir was killed. Rabia bin Rafi' caught Duraid and killed him, after which Prophet Muhammad ﷺ left for Ta'if to encounter the remaining defeated disbelievers. Booty was gained and later distributed amongst the Muslims. Seventy warriors from the opposition were killed and the rest captured, while the Muslims lost four companions to martyrdom.[283]

279 Surah Tawbah: 25.
280 Surah Tawbah: 26.
281 *Al-Rawd al-Unuf* 4/233.
282 *Zarqāni* 3/530.
283 *Zarqāni* 3/531.

GHAZWAH TA'IF

The leader of Banu Hawazin left Hunayn before Prophet Muhammad ﷺ reached Ta'if; he then locked himself in a fort which had supplies for years. The fort was later conquered and the people accepted Islam.

Type:	Expedition
Date:	13th Shawwal, 8AH
Opposition:	Banu Hawazin
No. of Muslims:	Unknown
No. of Unbelievers:	Unknown
Outcome:	Muslims gained victory

Ta'if is a very large city approximately two to three days' journey on foot from Makkah in the eastern direction. It is well-known for its fruits, such as figs, melons, raisins, grapes and pomegranates.[284] After escaping from the Battle of Hunayn, the Banu Thaqif and Hawazin sought asylum in Ta'if, making the city heavily populated with their presence.[285] Prophet Muhammad ﷺ gave the order for all booty and captives to be gathered in a location called Ji'ranah.[286]

284 Ibid 4/4-5.
285 *Al-Rahīq ul-Makhtūm* p.359.
286 *Zarqāni* 4/6.

• Buhran

ARABIA

•Ghuran

• Hunayn

• MAKKAH

Ta'if

Red Sea

Prophet Muhammad ﷺ despatched a troop with Khalid bin Walīd ؓ towards Ta'if while he ﷺ proceeded though Nakhla, Al-Yamaniyah and Laiyah.[287] At Laiyah there was a castle that belonged to Malik bin Awf, which the Prophet ﷺ gave orders to have destroyed. Thereafter, he ﷺ continued with his journey until he reached Ta'if, where he laid siege for approximately fourteen days according to Imam Muslim; however, historians have varied from ten to twenty.[288]

The Banu Thaqif were expert archers and after many fierce exchanges these encounters resulted in twelve companions being killed and several wounded.[289] For protection, the Muslims moved towards a higher location distanced from the castle which is now known as the Ta'if mosque.[290] A catapult was arranged by Prophet Muhammad ﷺ through Tufayl ad-Dausi ؓ when he returned from Sariyah Kaffayn.[291] He ﷺ encircled the town and used the catapult to fire rocks. Khalid bin Walīd ؓ challenged the archers on the roof to a one-to-one combat. They refused and proclaimed that it was futile as they had enough supplies for many years. Through the use of the catapult, the Muslims were successful in creating a pathway into the castle to set it on fire; however, in defence, the enemy began to strike the Muslims with hot iron, which again resulted in arrow shooting. Prophet Muhammad ﷺ ordered for the Muslims to retract and instead to cut down their trees and crops. This was later retracted as the people requested for the orchard trees to be spared.[292]

Later, another announcement was made by Prophet Muhammad ﷺ that if anyone exited the fort then he/she would be instantly freed. Upon this call, twenty-three men came out, and as promised, were set free.[293] Amidst the commotion Prophet Muhammad ﷺ saw a dream in which he was given a cup of milk. A fowl came and pecked at it, causing it to break. Prophet

287 *Al-Rahīq ul-Makhtūm* p.359.
288 Ibid.
289 *Zarqāni* 4/8.
290 Ibid p.9.
291 Ibid p.10.
292 *Al-Rahīq ul-Makhtūm* p.359.
293 Ibid p.360.

Muhammad ﷺ related the dream to Abu Bakr ؓ, who interpreted it to mean that the fort would not be conquered immediately, upon which he ﷺ replied, 'However, I do not think that.'[294] Prophet Muhammad ﷺ sought Nawfal bin Mu'awiyah al-Daylami ؓ who also interpreted dreams. He said, 'O Messenger of Allah ﷺ, it is similar to a fox in its den. If we remain, we will catch it. If we leave it, it will not cause harm to you.'[295]

Prophet Muhammad ﷺ ordered Umar ؓ to announce the order to return tomorrow morning, to which some Muslims remarked, 'Are we to leave without conquering the fort?' Thereafter, Prophet Muhammad ﷺ responded to their plea by staying to fight in the morning. As they engaged in combat in the morning they were wounded. When they were told to return again, they did so without complaint; this amused Prophet Muhammad ﷺ. The siege was lifted and Prophet Muhammad ﷺ remained in Ji'ranah for ten nights before distributing the booty.[296]

294 *Al-Rawd al-Unuf* 4/271.
295 *Al-Rahīq ul-Makhtūm* p.360.
296 Ibid.

GHAZWAH TABUK

Tabrani narrates on the authority of Imran bin Husayn that
the Christian Arabs wrote to Heraclius saying that Prophet
Muhammad ﷺ had passed away and people were dying from
drought. It was thus a very appropriate time to attack the Arabs.

Type:	Expedition
Date:	End of Rajab 9AH
Opposition:	The Romans
No. of Muslims:	30,000 men and 10,000 horses
Losses:	Unknown
No. of Unbelievers:	40,000 men
Losses:	Unknown
Prominent figures:	Heraclius
Outcome:	No combat

Tabuk is a popular region midway between Madinah towards
Jordan.[297] With the Muslims' increasing power and recognition of
their authority by rival factions, Caesar Heraclius could not over-
look their superiority in battle, nor could he ignore their grow-
ing numbers and popularity. In particular, Caesar feared that the
Muslims would become undefeatable. He decided to gather his
large army made up of the Byzantines and pro-Roman Ghassanid
tribes to attack Madinah.[298]

297 *Zarqāni* 4/65.
298 *Al-Rahīq ul-Makhtūm* p.368.

SYRIA

Dawmat ul-Jandal •

 Tabuk

ARABIA

Khaybar •

Red Sea

MADINAH •

When the news found its way to Madinah, it caused fear and commotion within the city. As the time drew near, the companions began preparations and were alert to the slightest of sounds. It was during these challenging times that the hypocrites planted their seed of hatred and evil against the Muslims. As narrated by Allah the Most High in Surah Tawbah:

$$وَٱلَّذِينَ ٱتَّخَذُواْ مَسْجِدًا ضِرَارًا و$$
$$كُفْرًا وَتَفْرِيقًا بَيْنَ ٱلْمُؤْمِنِينَ وَإِرْصَادًا لِّمَنْ حَارَبَ ٱللَّهَ وَرَسُولَهُۥ مِن قَبْلُ$$
$$وَلَيَحْلِفُنَّ إِنْ أَرَدْنَآ إِلَّا ٱلْحُسْنَىٰ وَٱللَّهُ يَشْهَدُ إِنَّهُمْ لَكَٰذِبُونَ$$

And as for those who take a mosque as a means of harming and disbelief, and to cause disunity between the Muslims and as an outpost for those who are in a war against Allah and His messenger prior, and they take an oath that they intend nothing but good, Allah bears witness that indeed they are liars.[299]

The hypocrites joined forces with the Byzantines to attack Madinah. Moreover, Abu Amir, the father of Hanzalah ﷺ, after Hawazin, paid a personal visit to the Byzantines with a heinous plan. He wrote a letter to the hypocrites of Madinah, requesting them to build a mosque not too far from Quba Mosque. Their excuse to Prophet Muhammad ﷺ was that it was tiresome and difficult to attend prayer in Quba Mosque due to the distance, hence the need for a mosque nearby. This was to be their hideout location and an area to store weapons to attack the Muslims. To avoid suspicion, they beseeched Prophet Muhammad's ﷺ presence in the Dirar Mosque and also requested him to lead a prayer for blessing. However, as Prophet Muhammad ﷺ was preparing for Tabuk he ﷺ delayed the visit till after his return.[300]

It was the month of Rajab in the year 9AH. As the heat of the scorching sun overpowered the land, the dates ripened and the trees became a source of shade and respite. Prophet Muhammad

299 Surah Tawbah: 107.
300 *Ma'riful Qur'an* Surah Tawbah.

led an army of Muslims towards the Byzantines to fight them. The Muslims decided to cross into the Byzantine vicinity before the Byzantines could enter the Arab land.[301] Amongst those who willingly accompanied Prophet Muhammad ﷺ for battle, there were those hypocrites who used excuses about the heat or the enemy. In response to their actions, Allah says in Surah Tawbah:[302]

$$فَرِحَ الْمُخَلَّفُونَ بِمَقْعَدِهِمْ خِلَافَ رَسُولِ اللَّهِ وَكَرِهُوا أَنْ يُجَاهِدُوا بِأَمْوَالِهِمْ$$
$$وَأَنْفُسِهِمْ فِي سَبِيلِ اللَّهِ وَقَالُوا لَا تَنْفِرُوا فِي الْحَرِّ قُلْ نَارُ جَهَنَّمَ أَشَدُّ حَرًّا$$
$$لَوْ كَانُوا يَفْقَهُونَ$$

Those who remained behind and rejoiced in being left behind Prophet Muhammad ﷺ, they hated to strive and fight for their wealth and themselves in the cause of Allah and they said: 'Do not go forth in this heat.' Say: 'The fire of Hell is more severe in heat,' if only they could comprehend.

When the order of Muhammad ﷺ echoed through Madinah, the valiant warriors marched towards the call of jihad. Tribes poured into Madinah to fight beside Prophet Muhammad ﷺ in battle, nor did they fall short in contributing towards the battle, whether through something small or large. Uthman bin Affan ؓ (may Allah accept his sincere efforts) provided immense support to the Muslim army. Uthman ؓ contributed two hundred ounces of gold in addition to the two hundred camels he had given for the journey to Syria. He later added another thousand dinars and presented it before Prophet Muhammad ﷺ.[303] Due to his excellence in action, Prophet Muhammad ﷺ prayed for him 'From this day onwards nothing will harm Uthman bin Affan.'[304] In the same manner, Abu Bakr ؓ devoted all his wealth to the cause of Allah, prioritising Allah and His Messenger over his own family. Umar

301 *Al-Rahīq ul-Makhtūm* p.370.
302 Surah Tawbah: 81.
303 *Zarqāni* 4/68-70, *Al-Rahīq ul-Makhtūm* p.371.
304 *Zarqāni* 4/71.

🌸 gave half his wealth towards the battle, and like so many others contributed towards the path of Allah without fear of poverty. May Allah accept all their efforts.

En route to Tabuk, leaving behind Ali 🌸 as his representative in Madinah and with the largest army of thirty thousand, Prophet Muhammad 🌸 reached a place called Al-Hijr, the residence of Thamud. During their stay, the Muslim army was prohibited from drinking the water of that area or even performing wudhu with it, due to the punishment that overpowered the people of Thamud.[305] It is also upon their arrival at the locality that the companions complained about the drought and their thirst. After Prophet Muhammad 🌸 made supplication, they were blessed with a cloud carrying rain, allowing them to drink to their full. During this trip, Prophet Muhammad 🌸 also warned the Muslims of a severe wind and so advised all to stay seated and to tie their camels. Unfortunately, a man stood amongst them and it is said he was blown to the Tai' mountain.[306] All of these incidents prove Prophet Muhammad's 🌸 prophethood and his status.

The army spent a total of twenty days in Tabuk. Despite the initial fears of danger from the Byzantines, it became evident that the rumors were unfounded. On the other hand, the promised conquest of Syria had not yet arrived. During this period, the Prophet entered into a treaty of peace with a Christian and Jewish community residing at the head of the Gulf of Aqabah and along its eastern coast. *Jizyah*[307] was also paid and security was promised regarding their borders.

Prophet Muhammad 🌸 returned to Madinah after fifty days, in the month of Ramadan. During this expedition, many Muslims stayed behind; among them were Ka'b bin Malik, Murarah bin ar-Rabi' and Hilal bin Ummayah. These individuals encountered a severe and difficult test from Allah. They were given an order by Prophet Muhammad 🌸 whereby they were restricted from being spoken to by anyone nor was anyone allowed to do business with

---

305 *Al-Rahīq ul-Makhtūm* pp.371-372.
306 Ibid.
307 A taxation which is paid by unbelievers in return for protection and freedom to practice their religion in an Islamic state.

them for fifty days.[308] After the lapse of this period, they were forgiven by Allah and his Prophet as mentioned by Allah in the Qur'an:

$$ وَعَلَى الثَّلَاثَةِ الَّذِينَ خُلِّفُواْ حَتَّى إِذَا ضَاقَتْ عَلَيْهِمُ الأَرْضُ بِمَا رَحُبَتْ وَضَاقَتْ عَلَيْهِمْ أَنفُسُهُمْ وَظَنُّواْ أَن لاَّ مَلْجَأَ مِنَ اللّهِ إِلاَّ إِلَيْهِ ثُمَّ تَابَ عَلَيْهِمْ لِيَتُوبُواْ إِنَّ اللّهَ هُوَ التَّوَّابُ الرَّحِيمُ $$

And as for the three who were left behind to the extent that the earth closed upon them despite its vastness and their souls confined them and they knew that there is no refuge from Allah except in Him. Then Allah turned to them so that they may repent. Indeed Allah is accepting of repentance, the Merciful.[309]

When their forgiveness was announced by Allah, all the companions rushed to notify them; indeed this was their happiest day. Upon his return, Prophet Muhammad ﷺ was also enlightened by Allah of the mischievous plans of the hypocrites regarding Masjid Dirar. Prophet Muhammad ﷺ immediately appointed two companions to go and demolish the masjid to ground level, and so the deed was carried out.

308 *Al-Rahīq ul-Makhtūm* p.375.
309 Surah Tawbah: 118.

BIBLIOGRAPHY

Allama Abu al-Qasim Abd al-Rahman ibn Abd Allah al-Suhayli, (2014) *Al-Rawd ul-Unuf, Al-Maktaba al-Assrya*, Volume 2-4.

Imam al-Zarqani (rah) (2004) *Al-Zarqani Sharh al-Mawahib, Markaz-e Ahle Sunnat Barkaat-e-Raza*, India. Volume 2-4.

Sheikh Safi Ar-Rahman Al-Mubarakpuri (rah), *Al-Rahīq ul-Makhtūm* (Arabic), Darusalam.

Sayyed Abul Hasan Alī Nadwi, (1993) *Qasas un-Nabiyeen* (Arabic), Majlis-e-Nashriyat-Islam.

Dr. Abu Khalil, *Atlas Sīrah tun Nabawiyyah* (Arabic), Daar ul-Fikr

Maulana Muhammad Shafi, *Ma'riful Qur'an*, Trans. Prof. Muhammad Hasan Asker and Prof. Muhammad Shamim, *Maktaba-e Darul Uloom*, Volume 7.

Imam ibn Diyai' (rah), *Tarīkh Makkah-tul Mukaramah wa Masjid al-Haram*, Daar ul-Kutub al-'Ilmiyyah.